SpringerBriefs in Education

We are delighted to announce SpringerBriefs in Education, an innovative product type that combines elements of both journals and books. Briefs present concise summaries of cutting-edge research and practical applications in education. Featuring compact volumes of 50 to 125 pages, the SpringerBriefs in Education allow authors to present their ideas and readers to absorb them with a minimal time investment. Briefs are published as part of Springer's eBook Collection. In addition, Briefs are available for individual print and electronic purchase.

SpringerBriefs in Education cover a broad range of educational fields such as: Science Education, Higher Education, Educational Psychology, Assessment & Evaluation, Language Education, Mathematics Education, Educational Technology, Medical Education and Educational Policy.

SpringerBriefs typically offer an outlet for:

- An introduction to a (sub)field in education summarizing and giving an overview of theories, issues, core concepts and/or key literature in a particular field
- A timely report of state-of-the art analytical techniques and instruments in the field of educational research
- A presentation of core educational concepts
- An overview of a testing and evaluation method
- A snapshot of a hot or emerging topic or policy change
- An in-depth case study
- A literature review
- A report/review study of a survey
- An elaborated thesis

Both solicited and unsolicited manuscripts are considered for publication in the SpringerBriefs in Education series. Potential authors are warmly invited to complete and submit the Briefs Author Proposal form. All projects will be submitted to editorial review by editorial advisors.

SpringerBriefs are characterized by expedited production schedules with the aim for publication 8 to 12 weeks after acceptance and fast, global electronic dissemination through our online platform SpringerLink. The standard concise author contracts guarantee that:

- an individual ISBN is assigned to each manuscript
- each manuscript is copyrighted in the name of the author
- the author retains the right to post the pre-publication version on his/her website or that of his/her institution

Noora J. Al-Thani · Zubair Ahmad

Teaching and Learning with Research Cognitive Theory

Unlocking Curiosity and Creativity for Problem-Solving Skills

Noora J. Al-Thani
Qatar University Young Scientists Center
(QUYSC)
Qatar University
Doha, Qatar

Zubair Ahmad
Qatar University Young Scientists Center
(QUYSC)
Qatar University
Doha, Qatar

ISSN 2211-1921 ISSN 2211-193X (electronic)
SpringerBriefs in Education
ISBN 978-3-031-87543-4 ISBN 978-3-031-87544-1 (eBook)
https://doi.org/10.1007/978-3-031-87544-1

This work was supported by Qatar National Library.
Open Access funding provided by the Qatar National Library.

© The Editor(s) (if applicable) and The Author(s) 2025. This book is an open access publication.

Open Access This book is licensed under the terms of the Creative Commons Attribution 4.0 International License (http://creativecommons.org/licenses/by/4.0/), which permits use, sharing, adaptation, distribution and reproduction in any medium or format, as long as you give appropriate credit to the original author(s) and the source, provide a link to the Creative Commons license and indicate if changes were made.
The images or other third party material in this book are included in the book's Creative Commons license, unless indicated otherwise in a credit line to the material. If material is not included in the book's Creative Commons license and your intended use is not permitted by statutory regulation or exceeds the permitted use, you will need to obtain permission directly from the copyright holder.
The use of general descriptive names, registered names, trademarks, service marks, etc. in this publication does not imply, even in the absence of a specific statement, that such names are exempt from the relevant protective laws and regulations and therefore free for general use.
The publisher, the authors and the editors are safe to assume that the advice and information in this book are believed to be true and accurate at the date of publication. Neither the publisher nor the authors or the editors give a warranty, expressed or implied, with respect to the material contained herein or for any errors or omissions that may have been made. The publisher remains neutral with regard to jurisdictional claims in published maps and institutional affiliations.

This Springer imprint is published by the registered company Springer Nature Switzerland AG
The registered company address is: Gewerbestrasse 11, 6330 Cham, Switzerland

If disposing of this product, please recycle the paper.

The original version of this book was revised by including the open access funding information and the logo.

Preamble

This book, *Teaching and Learning with Research Cognitive Theory*, serves as a comprehensive guide for educators, policymakers, and researchers dedicated to transforming educational practices through research-driven methodologies. Rooted in the foundational principles of Research Cognitive Theory (RCT), it bridges theoretical insights with practical applications, offering a cohesive framework to enhance teaching, learning, and professional development across all educational levels. By fostering a culture of inquiry and emphasizing evidence-based strategies, the book aspires to empower educators to cultivate research-driven environments, guide policymakers in crafting impactful educational frameworks, and inspire researchers to explore innovative intersections of pedagogy and cognitive development. The chapters collectively illuminate the pivotal role of research in reshaping educational experiences. The first chapter introduces the theoretical underpinnings of RCT, establishing its relevance in fostering independent, inquiry-based learning across various educational contexts. Chapters 2 and 3 delve into its application in primary and middle school settings, presenting actionable strategies like problem-based and project-based learning that engage younger learners in curiosity-driven exploration. These chapters underscore how RCT aligns with age-specific cognitive needs, laying a robust foundation for lifelong research skills.

The subsequent chapters transition into higher educational contexts. Chapter 4 emphasizes the transformative potential of multidisciplinary research experiences for high school students, illustrating how RCT enables learners to navigate complex, real-world challenges. Chapter 5 extends this exploration to undergraduate research, detailing how structured frameworks like CUREs (Course-Based Undergraduate Research Experiences) foster critical thinking, collaboration, and research proficiency in future professionals. Both chapters highlight the symbiotic relationship between dynamic research environments and cognitive development, positioning RCT as a cornerstone for academic and career success. The final chapter focuses on educators themselves, exploring how research can transform teacher education and professional development. It presents practical strategies for integrating RCT into teacher training programs and classroom practices, emphasizing the reciprocal influence between teacher competencies and student learning behaviors. This chapter also addresses the vital role of schools and policymakers in fostering research-centric cultures, ensuring that teachers are equipped to inspire inquiry and innovation in their students.

Together, these chapters form a coherent narrative that links theoretical foundations with real-world applications, demonstrating how RCT can revolutionize teaching and learning. Whether read as a guide for implementing research-driven pedagogies, a policy framework for educational reform, or a springboard for academic inquiry, this book offers a unifying vision of education as a dynamic, research-empowered endeavor. Through its comprehensive insights, it invites educators, policymakers, and researchers alike to collaboratively advance the frontiers of education, ensuring that learners and teachers are prepared for the complexities of the twenty-first century and beyond.

Competing Interests The authors have no competing interests to declare that are relevant to the content of this manuscript.

Contents

1 **Research Learning and Existing Theories in Learner Development** 1
   1.1 Different Aspects of Research and Its Learning Outcomes 2
      1.1.1 Knowledge Creation or Enhancement 3
      1.1.2 Fostering Research Attitude 4
      1.1.3 Cognitive Maturation of Research Skills 5
   1.2 Current Pedagogical Practices in RBL in Developing 21st-Century Skills 7
      1.2.1 Learning Through Independent Research 8
      1.2.2 Learning Through Integrated/Embedded Research 9
   1.3 Learning Models and Underlying Theories in Research Learning 10
   1.4 Chapter Summary 18
   Glossary 20
   References 21

2 **The Scope of Problem-Based Learning and Integrated Research Education for Primary Learners** 25
   2.1 Fostering Curiosity Through Research-Driven Inquiry 26
   2.2 What is Scientific Inquiry? 28
   2.3 The Relationship Between Scientific Inquiry and Problem-Solving Skills 33
   2.4 Unraveling the Influence of Digital Technology on Research and Problem-Based Learning in Primary Skills 35
   2.5 Chapter Summary 38
   Glossary 39

	References	40
3	**Driving Project-Based Learning and Problem-Based Learning Through Research in Middle Schools**	45
	3.1 Project-Based Learning and Problem-Based Learning in Middle Schools	45
	3.2 The Integration of Research Cognitive Theory (RCT) into PjBL and PBL	49
	3.3 Educational Technology's Role in PjBL and PBL	50
	3.4 Challenges and Opportunities in Implementation and Assessment Strategies	52
	3.5 Chapter Summary	54
	Glossary	55
	References	56
4	**Revolutionizing RCT in Highschool Through Research Experiences**	59
	4.1 Theory of Revolutionizing RCT Through Dynamic Real-World Experiential Research for Pre-University Students	60
	4.2 Multidisciplinary Research Experience and Research Cognitive Behavior	62
	4.2.1 Why a Dynamic Multidisciplinary Research Experience?	62
	4.2.2 Multidisciplinary Chemistry-Based High School Research Experience (CHSRE) Program Implementing the Research Cognitive Theory	63
	4.2.3 Instructional Design of the CHSRE Model	65
	4.3 Near Peer Mentoring Model in a Dynamic High School Research Environment	66
	4.3.1 Why the Near Peer Mentoring Model?	66
	4.4 Learning Through "Research Cognitive Theory" for High School Research Experiences	68
	4.5 Chapter Summary	73
	Glossary	74
	References	76
5	**Transforming Undergraduate Research Experiences Through RCT**	81
	5.1 Research Cognitive Behavior Development in an Undergraduate Research Environment	82
	5.2 Course-based Undergraduate Research Experiences (CURE) Model and Adaptation of RCT to Enhance Work Readiness	84
	5.3 RCT in CURE Based Research Internship Programs	88
	5.4 Chapter Summary	91
	Glossary	92
	References	93

6	**Teaching Research to Teachers—Traversing from Research-Oriented Education to Research Learning Theory**	97
	6.1 Research-Based Teacher Education Practices	97
	6.2 Professional Development Experiences in Integrating Research-Based Learning in K-12 Classrooms	99
	6.3 How Can Schools Support the Promotion of Research Education Training of Teachers?	104
	6.4 Relationship Between Teacher Competencies and Student Learning Behavior in the Context of Research Learning	107
	6.5 Chapter Summary	109
	Glossary	110
	References	111
Appendices		113

Chapter 1
Research Learning and Existing Theories in Learner Development

Abstract This chapter, titled "Research Learning and Existing Theories in Learner Development," delves into the comprehensive role of RL in shaping learner attitudes, skills, and knowledge. It outlines how research processes—ranging from identifying key investigation areas to disseminating findings—contribute to developing contextual, technical, and cognitive knowledge. The chapter underscores the importance of fostering a positive research attitude, which encompasses interest and aspirations, rooted in Bandura's Social Learning Theory (SLT) and Social Cognitive Learning Theory (SCLT). The book presents two primary RL models: Learning through Independent Research and Learning through Integrated/Embedded Research. These models are examined in the context of their historical evolution, pedagogical practices, and their ability to cater to different educational tiers, from primary school to university levels. The discussion extends to various RL frameworks, notably the Research Skill Development (RSD) Framework and Course-based Undergraduate Research Experiences (CUREs), highlighting their effectiveness in enhancing research skills, self-efficacy, and career aspirations. Furthermore, the chapter introduces the proposed Research Cognitive Theory (RCT), an extension of SCT, emphasizing the dynamic research environment's role in intellectual and cognitive development. RCT postulates that intellectual learning occurs through reciprocal interactions within a research community, fostering intrinsic motivation, research self-efficacy, and various cognitive and research skills. The chapter outlines key RCT components, including self-efficacy, behavioral capability, expectations, self-control, observational learning, and reinforcements. This book aims to provide educators, researchers, and policymakers with a profound understanding of the transformative power of RL in developing 21st-century skills. By integrating empirical evidence and theoretical insights, it advocates for structured, dynamic research environments that challenge and motivate learners, thereby ensuring long-term intellectual and cognitive growth.

Keywords Research Cognitive Theory (RCT) · Inquiry-Based Learning (IBL) · Cognitive development · Research attitude · Knowledge creation

1.1 Different Aspects of Research and Its Learning Outcomes

Research is defined as a systematic process of carrying out an investigation/inquiry, by gathering adequate information, performing a detailed assessment of the obtained information, and carefully laying out the optimum conclusions on the raised inquiry/investigation, thereby resulting in the new generation of ideas and/or solutions (Apps, 1972). By carrying out the different procedures in research, an individual experiences curiosity, and exhibits inquiry, critical thinking, and problem-solving capabilities, thereby resulting in innovation and creativity. Hence, we could also say that "carrying out research" can subject an individual to developing/nurturing certain dispositions that are deemed quintessential in the different learner development phases. These dispositions or skills often shape the attitude of the learners in a particular direction while being subjected to different engaging environments. It is also vital to realize that the skills and attitudes together frame the cognitive and psychosocial readiness of a learner and hence, we may not be able to overlook the role of research-integrated/based learning in a child's educational environment. Diverse research studies have also emphasized the significance of developing these skills for improving an individual's assessment ability to make critical decisions at the appropriate time (Puerta et al., 2016). Irrespective of the diversity in disciplines, research is highly commended as a learning experience and teaching method for developing a learner's overall development.

Research, either basic or applied, is often practiced/taught in two different learning schemes—learning through independent research and learning through integrated/embedded research (Christophorou & Hunter, 1984). Often Research learning can be observed to be addressed as research on the process of learning. However, we would like to employ the term, "Research learning" (RL) as the process of learning by/through research. We can also elaborately describe RL as an acquisition of knowledge and skills by practicing systematic research.

On exploring the diverse approaches in teaching research, both formal and informal learning environments have been constructed and assigned for young learners to experience and learn through different research learning practices. Eventually, despite the learning methods, the goal of research learning is often streamlined to foster learner readiness levels that include knowledge, attitudes, and skills. The learner readiness measures, in this book will be portrayed as physical (knowledge), cognitive (skills), and psychological (attitudes, values). Now we may discuss how research leads to physical, cognitive, and psychosocial maturation or learner readiness.

While we discuss the aspects of acquiring learner readiness or outcomes through research learning, we will have to prompt the different steps that are carried out while performing research, which indeed will elaborate on how each step of research can contribute to each aspect. **This is crucial as we aim through this book, to understand and establish the relationship between research practice and cognitive**

1.1 Different Aspects of Research and Its Learning Outcomes

Fig. 1.1 The Fundamental Steps of Research Methodology. This figure outlines the sequential stages of the research process, emphasizing key elements such as inquiry formulation, data collection, and analysis, which align with Research Cognitive Theory (RCT) principles like self-regulation and critical thinking. Figure by authors

development. The basic steps that are carried out during research (see Fig. 1.1) can be summarized as below:

- Identifying the key focus of the investigation
- Performing a background check
- Designing the execution or research plan
- Gathering relevant data
- Performing systematic evaluation and analysis
- Draw meaningful and profound conclusions.
- Dissemination of the study/research outcomes

We will be hereafter discussing each individual aspect of learner readiness, i.e. knowledge, attitude/values, and skills based on the process that is entailed during each step of research.

1.1.1 Knowledge Creation or Enhancement

Universally, research is carried out in the research and development sector of industries or at university premises with the active collaboration of researchers, industrial representatives, and academic faculty along with young scholars. While research at university premises involves young talent pool who apprentice the academicians with unlimited access to intellectual capital, it becomes a favorable venue for research learning. Hence as Goddard (1998) states, universities have been recognized as knowledge-based organizations that involve key knowledge processes like knowledge development, learning, and knowledge dissemination. In fact, these processes ideally project the social usefulness of performing research, by encompassing the situated knowledge (Cunliffe, 2020). During the investigation of a research project, the scholars engage in sharing both conceptual and practical forms of knowledge and expertise (MacIntosh et al., 2012). They rely on people's contextualized work experiences to draw out their research investigation key areas/problems and nurture an ability to develop knowledge in ambiguous and fluid situations of lived experience.

Research learning can profoundly lead to knowledge empowerment in terms of knowledge development under variant aspects like contextual understanding, technical knowledge and cognitive knowledge. Contextual knowledge is the deeper understanding that a learner can gain in the context of his/her learner's experience. For example, when a material science student understands the different molecular compositions of a polymer, the knowledge generated is contextual knowledge. Meanwhile, when the student gains knowledge in performing the steps to operate lab equipments, the knowledge generated is generally addressed as technical knowledge. On the other hand, the knowledge that students acquire in analyzing molecular composition is referred to as cognitive knowledge. Though they can be distinctly defined in categorization, their objective is also bound to certain grey areas, as the impact of learner experience is not limited to any one knowledge category. While contextual knowledge and technical knowledge can aid them in their university or educational stages, cognitive knowledge indeed guarantees better employment and living conditions apart from the former two. Meanwhile, knowledge generation could also be categorized as explicit (knowledge gained/recorded), implicit (knowledge within), and tacit (experiential/unrecorded). It is interesting to observe that research learning is performed on a tacit understanding by employing the implicit knowledge of the involved personnel to create explicit knowledge. RL contributes an alliance of all knowledge elements with an ultimate delivery of explicit knowledge. This knowledge is later taken as an attitude, as it is the representation of one's own attitude of understanding that fact.

1.1.2 Fostering Research Attitude

Attitude is often explained by psychologists as an outlook of an individual in evaluating something or someone (Bain, 1928). It can also be termed as a tendency to engage positively or negatively toward a specific idea, object, person, or situation. When an individual expresses their outlook on performing or experiencing any/all of the aspects of research, this tendency is termed as research attitude. The growth of attitude in individuals is attributed to their psychological strength.

There are different discussions on the relationship between knowledge and attitude. As we stated earlier, explicit knowledge becomes an attitude, especially in the case of research learning. There is diverse empirical evidence that sheds light on the distinct relationship between interest, aspiration, and attitude. Research interest and aspiration are the often-studied elements associated with research attitudes. These studies were framed on the foundations of Bandura's social learning theory, social cognitive learning theory and social career cognitive theory (Bandura, 2002). As students perform the different steps of research and a sense of achievement invades them, positive tendencies seem to develop. As attitude is a broader dimension, interest and aspiration are a more subjective term that stems from an attitude. So far, studies have been focused on research interests and aspirations and not explicitly on research attitudes, we portray research attitudes mostly based on two main aspects - research interest and research aspirations. Significant volume of research findings portray the positive relationship between students' research interest and their research experiences (Ghanem et al., 2018; Holme, 1994; Hunter et al., 2007; Jones et al., 2010; Knight & Botting, 2016; Kubisch et al., 2021; Laursen et al., 2010; Leontovich,

2003). These studies have discussed the development of student's research interests that stemmed from RL driven/integrated activities regardless of the disciplines or pedagogies adopted in delivering these research experiences. Many programs like university research programs, school research programs, field-based research programs, or course-based research programs have all been validated in developing research interests. High school and university research experiences are the main contributing agents of a positive research attitude. RL through university research experiences has been demonstrated to affect student aspirations for higher education and careers in research-based fields. They have a role in partaking in the development of student awareness of different research-based career options, thereby creating clarity in their career choices and therefore prompting them to prepare for graduate education. We will be detailing the depth of building attitude in the later sections whereby we discuss the different theories associated with research learning.

1.1.3 Cognitive Maturation of Research Skills

Cognitive development or maturation is one of the main outcomes of RL that makes RL highly favored among current educators. As the 21st century demands learners and young employees to be superior in critical thinking, problem-solving, creativity, collaboration, decision-making, and analytical interpretation, RL provides the ideal platform for learners to experience and acknowledge. Research participation can foster communication capabilities and critical thinking skills as the learners involve themselves in understanding diverse research processes in a collaborative research environment. Arguably, the most well-documented and thoroughly examined outcome of RL experiences is their influence on the development of researchers' abilities and competencies in performing research-related tasks, including data entry, analysis, interpretation, and a range of laboratory techniques and procedures. Learners sharpen their ability to think as they regularly practice finding answers to the endless questions encountered during the different stages of research. For example, Hunter et al. (2007), as well as Laursen et al. (2010) record that student involvement in research can promote their cognitive growth and professional socialization thereby enhancing their confidence to do research. This confidence is also associated with building self-efficacy, which indeed has been discussed by many researchers while associating it with heightening career aspirations. This connection was identified through a study grounded in the Social Cognitive Career Theory (Lent et al., 1994, 2000, 2005) which offers a valuable framework for examining potential logical and sequential relationships between students' skill and knowledge acquisition, their self-efficacy, and their aspirations.

Another perspective of dissecting the development of cognitive gains through research is that during the RL process, the learners view, read, decide, and act critically, through a concise analysis, and synthesis of complex ideas. This cognitive ability of analytical thinking is essential for reaching a feasible consensus while framing a research question, and parallelly exercising problem-solving and decision-making. During the process, learners foster information literacy skills while accessing and synthesizing information from various sources. This capability to acquire relevant information has proven to be valuable not only for scholarly outcomes but also for workplace and career success. These skills are highly demanded by the job market and therefore easily transferable to not only various academic disciplines but also to different career fields. Another important cognitive capability that needs to be nurtured from an early age and of greater significance is creativity, which in fact is a highly in-demand workplace disposition. We would also emphasize creativity as cross cognitive ability as it needs to be displayed not only for creative outcomes but also in integrated dimensions of problem-solving and analytical thinking. RL subject learners to explore creative approaches to problem-solving thereby leading to blooming novelty and innovation laid-out solutions. Creative researchers learn to question the status quo, pitch in new ideas, and apply innovative solutions to challenges.

Collaboration and communication are two main cognitive pillars that stem from a research environment (Michael et al., 2013). Both cognitive pillars are essential in all learner development stages, as a young toddler transcends from a child to a fully mature scholar. No other learning environment can develop these cognitive pillars to the optimum other than research-based environments, as a multitude of peer collaboration is evident across diverse demographics. RL in addition, engages learners in presenting findings and carrying out discussions with peers and mentors. This leads the learners to smoothen their communication, cultivating the ability to articulate ideas, listen actively, and initiate constructive dialogue. Collaboration and communication work conjointly across different age groups, continents, ethnicities, cultures, and languages in a research space as a project lifts off. Even while narrowing the research premises to certain demographic groups, we cannot overlook both the skills of being richly cultured. We believe that these two skills are also the most crucial skills for public outreach, either while disseminating the results or for the commercialization of any service or product.

Research often requires diverse approaches like integrated approaches, that encourage learners to explore newer horizons. An inter-disciplinary or multi-disciplinary or transdisciplinary approach will train the learners to connect ideas and traverse through different fields. This characteristic of research practice promotes cognitive flexibility, resilience, and adaptability in addressing complex dimensions. Interdisciplinary research learning offers the key solution to improve the perspectives through which one envisions the project problems, aims, objectives, and solutions. This in turn is also a critical contributor to the development of creativity.

Apart from the 4Cs—Communication, collaboration, creativity, critical thinking, and the other 21st-century skills like problem-solving, and logical reasoning, the learners are also adept to organizational/workplace skills. Running the feasibility test of research methods, and planning the methodology with optimum data collection instruments, and analysis schemes enhance learners' planning abilities. The learners do experience the stages of project planning and management as they familiarize themselves with research plans and evaluate its feasibility. The research planning and coordination is mostly performed by university students rather than school students. Self-efficacy is also one of the important organizational skills that are developed as the learners carry out research activities. This is built on the effect of interest and skills that all together build confidence and pave the belief in learners to perform activities independently. Self-efficacy is a very significant trait demanded by employers who require employees to work with less supervision. As self-efficacy is defined as the individual's self-belief in executing a particular task, it categorically falls under attitude. However, the term also strikes on the individual's ability to execute/perform as an effect of interest, thereby placing it under cognitive aspects. Experiencing research learning can boost learners' self-efficacy to accomplish goals. Research activities also promote challenges wherein the learners need to take initiative, manage their time, and work independently and effectively. Empathy and sensitivity are traits that are often observed in researchers who can connect the relevance of social issues and put their focus of research into providing tangible solutions to these issues. As learners can be exposed to diverse social and contextual phenomena during RL activities, they also develop tolerance, a sense of belonging, and values that are much required for the stability and empowerment of society.

1.2 Current Pedagogical Practices in RBL in Developing 21st-Century Skills

We believe RL has evolved gradually in the last century according to the needs and requirements of the respective eras. In the early 20th century, research learning was only practiced among university researchers and their apprentices. This apprenticeship model has still managed to transcend to the 21st century, thereby witnessing a surge in the researcher career domain. Despite the advancement of different teaching practices and pedagogies, this apprenticeship model has significantly managed to stand apart from the rest of the RL approaches. Research based learning has climbed and subsided since Dewey prompted educators to ponder different exploratory learning models for all learner groups (Dewey, 1997). The surges can also be attributed to the post-Sputnik discovery mode of learning (Barrow, 2006), thereby embedding it in the curriculum. RBL has been followed across all educational tiers commencing from primary school (Hmelo-Silver et al., 2007) to the university levels (Boyer, 1990). Undergraduate research is strongly and widely adopted across many universities either as informal research experience programs or embedded in the course curriculum as course-based research experience programs. Though Hmelo-Silver et al. (2007) strongly vouched for learner outcomes as an effect of RBL, Hunter et al. (2007) do not agree upon it. For example, RBL and its positive learner outcomes were found by Camacho et al. (2017), after conducting a literature review and empirically by Mellander and Svärdh (2018) with a large-scale longitudinal study.

Despite the haze on the effect of RBL on learner development, research as a process for student learning through inquiry based learning has become progressively widespread in undergraduate degrees and graduate coursework (Etzkowitz, 2003). Research processes through inquiry have conventionally not been made explicit at the undergraduate level may be due, in part, to the conceptual difficulties faced by educators when facilitating complex learning with large numbers of learners, and a large proportion of those learners are underprepared for research responsibilities (Lazonder & Harmsen, 2016). The lapse in the students' rigor during their undergraduate study is also an added educational risk for RBL. To mitigate this risk, a consistent, scaffolded approach may be needed to guide students toward increasing rigor and aptitude. According to Lazonder and Harmsen (2016), a guided process can only help students understand and articulate the development of their research skills. We believe that each approach has its own pros and cons. Based on our understanding of the different RL approaches, we have categorized RL under 2 main themes.

1. Learning through independent research
2. Learning through integrated/embedded research

We will be discussing these two different approaches in detail hereafter.

1.2.1 Learning Through Independent Research

This model could be referred to as the oldest RL model as research learning was preached and carried out along the same timeline as that of the research. The process of learning happens through a natural phenomenon, whereby a learner or an apprentice masters the research skills by following the instructions set forward by the lead researcher. This model also could be referred to as the apprenticeship model. Sadler and his research team vouches this model as the most ideal educational approach given that in the earlier times, graduate learners aspired to be professional scientists initially joined an apprentice (Sadler et al., 2010). With this model, RL occurred in a linear method of instruction, wherein the learners initially performed peripheral activities of the research, meanwhile, they took hold of central activities as time and skill progressed. An apprentice may initially be involved in peripheral activities such as cleaning apparatus, preparing samples, or reading data. As they become more experienced with the equipment, tools, protocols, and laboratory, their activities become specific and central. Thereby, the apprentice progresses to independently designing and conducting their own experiments and may even take on the responsibility of mentoring newer members of the laboratory community (Burgin & Sadler, 2016). Though this model is successful with graduate learners, it is evident that it is mostly suited to the profile of the upper layers of the educational tier, who were more focused on mastering skills and knowledge to conquer a specific domain. Though this model was adopted in younger educational stages like middle school, and high school, the learning process could not be tended to be productive in terms of nurturing research skills, knowledge, or attitudes (Barab & Hay, 2001). This model was basically employed to cultivate school students' subject interest and the activities were designed or structured to function within a time frame (like during summer breaks).

1.2 Current Pedagogical Practices in RBL in Developing 21st-Century Skills

We believe multiple factors like time restrictions, the generation gap between the faculty and young learners, issues with learner reachability, and informal learning settings have contributed to the convergence of this model's outcomes. However, owing to the knowledge surge in the context of teaching pedagogies and research in learner development, educators were strict on exercising RL at a younger educational tier, thereby leading to the evolution of the next two models. The apprenticeship model also depicted another limitation that was evident among all the learner stages, which was the quantitative impact of the model. This model could only focus on a limited number of students, who were intellectually and academically higher than their peers. On the other hand, this RL model was also limited to the development of research skills and careers.

1.2.2 Learning Through Integrated/Embedded Research

As time progressed and the research issues were more generalized, Integrated Research learning approaches were designed to cater to cross-disciplinary context. This approach was implemented in the late 20th century, when RL was considered one of the objectives of learning, and research skills were adopted by all domains. During this period, diverse informal and formal teaching practices were launched as part of the educational revolution to mold the learners as deemed fit for the industrial revolution and computer age (Adedokun & Adedokun et al., 2012; Albareda-Tiana et al., 2018; Al-Thani et al., 2020, 2022; Burgess, 2011). RL was practiced through different integrated pedagogies like inquiry-based learning (IBL), project-based learning (PjBL), and problem-based learning (PBL). These pedagogies were mainly developed to foster scientific skills in students and research skills were deemed to be inevitable in the scientific context. School-based research learners are not typically subjected to the real-world research with the mentorship of research scientists in a few of these informal pedagogies, and thus schoolteachers and project leaders carry them through any or all of the diverse research learning steps that involve inquiry, investigation, problem-solving, innovation, designing, and dissemination. The educators mirror RL steps to establish a scientific methodology during project execution thereby ensuring maximum productivity with minimum risks. RL in this approach was considered more to accommodate a broader spectrum to impact a larger audience through a designed curriculum or learning framework. As learners practice RL through this model, they are able to work in interdisciplinary, or multidisciplinary contexts that merge two or more different disciplines, thereby prompting learners to develop divergent thinking from RL. School students especially primary, middle, and high school students are recently engaged in the embedded research learning model, as the curriculum standards outline learning experiences that are research-based laboratory activities (McMiller et al., 2006; Meerah & Arsad, 2010; Sabirova & Zakirova, 2015). The curriculum standards are focused more on learner outcomes and hence RL is easily adapted to the school classrooms.

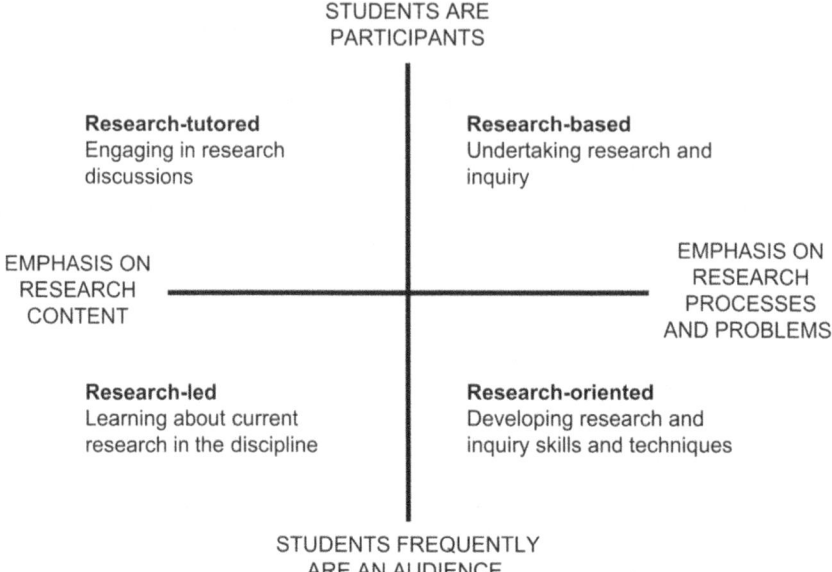

Fig. 1.2 Visualizing the links between curriculum design and the research–teaching nexus. This figure demonstrates how curriculum elements align with key components of Research Cognitive Theory (RCT), including fostering self-efficacy, observational learning, and reflective practice. Reproduced with permission licensed under CC BY 4.0 (Vereijken et al., 2018)

Despite the added benefits of a wide reachability of research learners, we should also consider the limitations in this model. According to (Healey & Jenkins, 2009), representation of curriculum links to research teaching design, there exists a thin line of uncertainty on learner participation (see Fig. 1.2). For example, in the case of inquiry-based learning, learners are actively involved as participants when the learning experiences revolve around research discussions or carrying out research and inquiry to solve research problems. Meanwhile, learners go passive when learning experiences are more contextual and focus on developing skills and techniques.

1.3 Learning Models and Underlying Theories in Research Learning

RL practices and approaches were developed based on different learning theories and models. RL has evolved through the evidence and impact of different models and frameworks that have been developed and practiced with the core objective of equipping learners with different research skills. One of the most prominent model is the Research Skill Development Framework by Willison and O'Regan that was developed to help educators formulate pedagogies that support RL through research

1.3 Learning Models and Underlying Theories in Research Learning

(Willison & O'Regan, 2007). This framework systematically outlines the foundational processes, providing educators with a structured approach to fostering undergraduate research capabilities. While the RSD framework is not a one-size-fits-all solution, it emphasizes the importance of educators tailoring its application to cultivate students' abilities in research, critical analysis, and problem-solving. By doing so, it supports the broader goal of equipping learners with skills that contribute to their ongoing personal and professional development throughout life.

The RSD framework is represented as a matrix of six components of research processes, that involves the researcher's capability to inquire, to apply proper methodology, to critically evaluate, organize and synthesize information, and to properly transfer knowledge through effective communication distributed, along five levels of student autonomy (aptitude) as shown in the Fig. 1.3.

The six facets represent the 'what' in research question and the range of autonomy comprises five levels, from closed and prescribed to open-ended research processes. The five levels indicate on 'how' to teach the skills. The five levels represent the five degrees of autonomy that intricate scaffolding courses along a range from 'Prescribed Research' (where learners are directed and protocoled) to 'Unbounded Research' (where learners have a high degree of freedom in initiating and deciding research

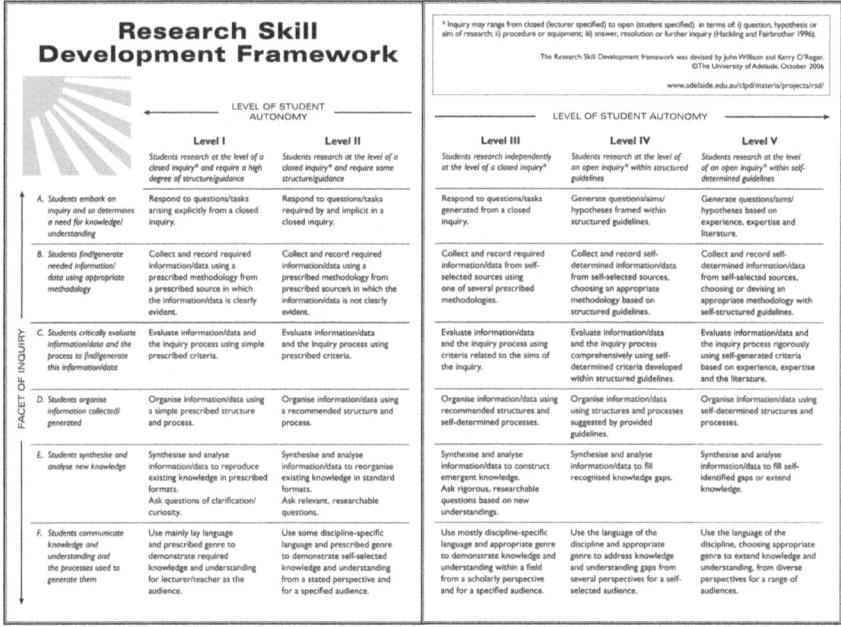

Fig. 1.3 The five level RSD framework. It outlines a structured approach to fostering research skills in learners through levels of cognitive autonomy. It provides a progressive model for developing inquiry-based competencies, from dependent guidance to independent research, ensuring adaptability across disciplines and educational settings. Reproduced with permission from Willison and O'Regan (2007). Copyright Taylor & Francis, 2007

directions). The RSD framework has been employed by academics in multiple courses across undergraduate disciplines and implemented as a model for analysis of learner thinking and development, at gender-based and employer-employee difference studies.

Another significant model that is extensively incorporated across different research learning activities and across diverse disciplines is the Course-based undergraduate research experiences (CUREs). They were initially employed by university faculty to train undergraduates in scientific research. CURE model-based research has proven to be as effective as the apprenticeship model research experiences that are normally practiced by UG students. CUREs pose numerous pros over traditional laboratory courses and research internships. They are capable of engaging many students at one time, and as it is course based, all enrolled students are able to participate (Auchincloss et al., 2014). CUREs have five defining characteristics that are integrated into the laboratory-based course curriculum. The elements feature discovery, iteration, collaboration, scientific experience, and dissemination. CURE study reports have identified UG student gains in research skills, self-efficacy, and college persistence. CUREs provide students with an opportunity to engage in a distinctive blend of activities, fostering gradual attainment of a wide range of cognitive, social, and behavioral skills and outcomes. See Figure 1.4 for the Four-step CURE Pedagogical Framework used to develop and implement CURES. Appendix A details these stages to indicate their impact on learners.

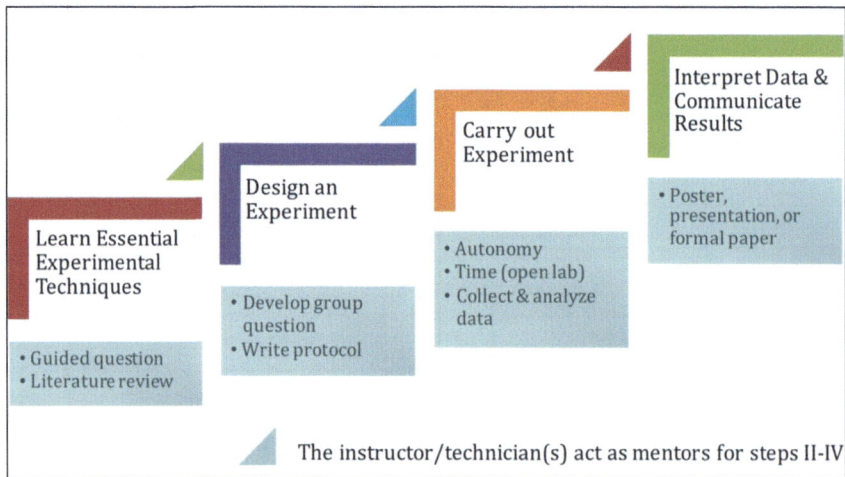

Fig. 1.4 The four-step CURE pedagogical framework. This framework outlines the sequential stages of designing and implementing Course-based Undergraduate Research Experiences (CUREs). The steps include identifying research questions, engaging in inquiry-based learning, analyzing data, and disseminating findings, aligning with RCT principles such as observational learning, self-efficacy, and collaborative inquiry. Reproduced with permission from (McLaughlin et al., 2017). Copyright Taylor & Francis, 2017

CURE model has been adapted and revised regularly according to the faculty perspectives and student learning demands. Though, CURE was initially introduced in biology courses at university level, and was extensively practiced in science classrooms, it is recently gaining popularity among social science researchers whereby the model has proven effective in enhancing understanding research processes and ethics, self-confidence, perseverance, collaboration and also developing their graduate career aspirations (Ruth et al., 2023).

Last decade has also witnessed the effect of research experience model on high school students as different programs like High School Summer Research Program (HSSRP) which was launched in 2013 at the University of California—Los Angeles (UCLA) Henry Samueli School of Engineering and Applied Sciences (Kittur et al., 2017). Students perform an 8-week research in engineering domains where they are trained to disseminate their research findings through scientific posters, and oral presentations. They adopt a "learn-by-teaching" system that further subjects all students to the multitude of creative strategies that are currently employed across the engineering disciplines to tackle world issues. This model also portrayed a positive effect with a high likelihood of pursuing a STEM (Science, Technology, Engineering and Mathematics) degree and advanced STEM degrees. We also developed chemistry-based high school Research Experience model (CHSRE) in 2022 based on a 12-year high school research program (Al-Thani et al., 2022). Our 2-month research program was mainly focused on building research competencies and attitudes and hence, careful study was performed on the environment that was structured to witness a gradual but solid change in student behavior. Hence the study period was also based on five-year alumni students' feedback that offered the retaining impact of the program on the research skills and attitudes. The detailed conceptual framework of the study will be deeply discussed in Chap. 4.

As the educational tier lowers, we have observed that very limited studies are recorded to depict the research learning in middle school students that focus on research skills. One study reports the inclusion of middle school students in laboratory based summer internship, which engaged students in research activities (McMiller et al., 2006). This study, however, delved into the deepening of students' understanding about the interdisciplinary nature without focusing on the student behavior or attitudes. We have also recognized that as we move down along the educational tier, educators employ research settings like lab-based projects and internships in the view of developing any one or more outcomes of research rather than research careers, or aspirations or research interest. For example, evidence suggests that primary students are mostly introduced to inquiry driven curiosity and problem solving, whereas middle school students apply inquiry driven, problem based, project-based innovation. As a student reaches pre-university, research aspirations, and research competencies also come into the light. It is also understood that research skills are fully required as the students mature to the level of practicing open research, as practiced during undergraduate experience. We believe that a constructivist approach henceforth guides the research learning process to ripen the research skills, competencies, and contextual knowledge.

There are multiple learning theories that have led to the maturation of research learning since the last century. In the sections below, we will be introducing the different theories that have contributed to the instructional design in research learning. As research was practiced and its instructional design was passed on to the apprentices, the theoretical framework behind the apprenticeship model was based on social learning theory (SLT), a two-dimensional approach, where learning is articulated as the result of behavior based on observation (Guile & Young, 1998). According to the SLT, research apprenticeships gain his skills and expertise based on his experiences with the research environment and the research lead. This observational process that is involved in establishing this learning process is mainly focused on four basic aspects—attention, retention, reproduction, motivation.

SLT was promptly adopted and promoted for observing desirable behavioral change in the target individual involved in the process of learning. According to this theory, we learn from our association and interaction with the surrounding individuals. This theory does not establish the effect of intrinsic motivation in an individual on his ability to learn from the people around him. It is mostly observational as people develop similar behaviors as they regularly observe people. Bandura advocates on the effect of imitation that engages reproduction of motor activities (Bandura, 1971). SLT is the most researched and influential learning theory in learning and development. The basic concepts of traditional learning theory are embedded with the concepts of social learning theory. This theory is an intermediary bridge between behaviorist learning theories and cognitive learning theories because it incorporates attention, memory, and motivation. Bandura also believes that a direct reinforcement cannot account for all types of learning and hence, he considered the social aspect, arguing that people can learn and develop their behavior by watching other people. According to SLT (Bandura, 1971), learning is a cognitive process, reliant on mental processing and construction, which occurs in a social context through observing and interacting with others. Situated-learning theory is a form of social learning theory that emphasizes the importance of situating learning in an authentic activity, context, and culture (Brown et al., 1989; Lave & Wenger, 1991). In the earlier research context, most of the studies explored the concept of research training environment and research skills based on social learning theory and situated learning theory. Students do the work that scientists do (e.g., ask questions, design studies, collect and analyze data, build models) in the context of a real scientific problem or question, in which the solution or answer is unknown. This situation is created in the form of research settings thereby driving inquiry to experience for developing knowledge and skills. Research learning therefore feathers from the same flock of social learning theory and situation learning theory. See Figure 1.5 for the SLT modeling process.

As we analyze the behavior of an individual learner, we observe that in the case of developing research learning outcomes, Bandura's Social learning theory has certain limitations. It does not reflect on the multi-dimensional aspects of cognitive development. Recent investigations into the research associated with research experience programs reflect the adoption of Bandura's Social Cognitive learning theory, thereby offering deeper insights into the cognitive behavior associated with research experiences. While SLT posits learning takes place through observation, imitation,

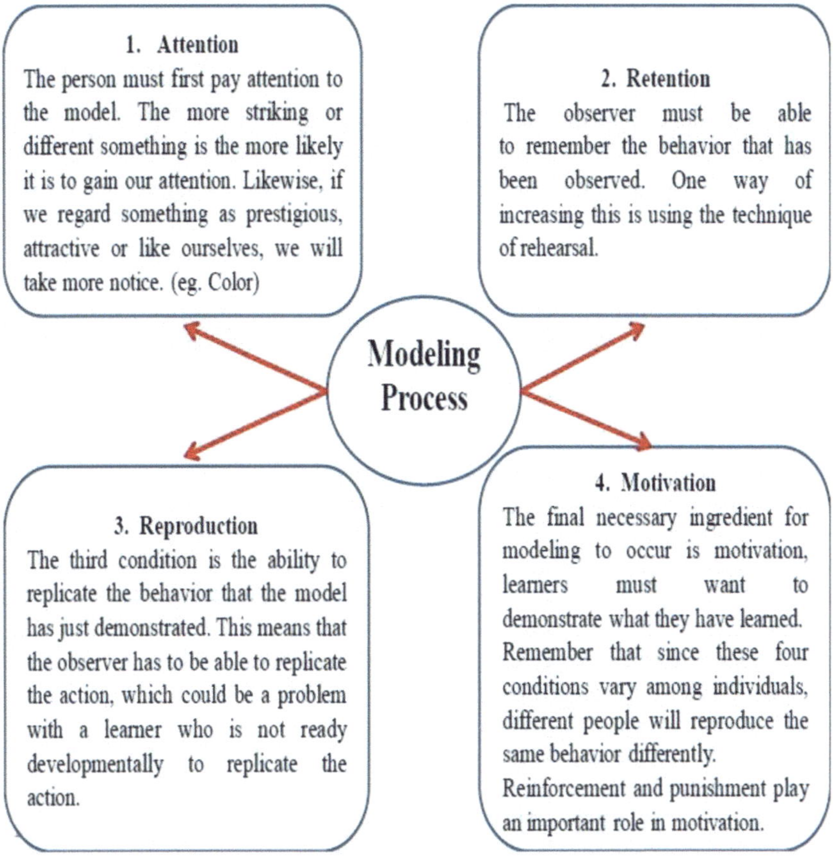

1.3 Learning Models and Underlying Theories in Research Learning

1. Attention
The person must first pay attention to the model. The more striking or different something is the more likely it is to gain our attention. Likewise, if we regard something as prestigious, attractive or like ourselves, we will take more notice. (eg. Color)

2. Retention
The observer must be able to remember the behavior that has been observed. One way of increasing this is using the technique of rehearsal.

Modeling Process

3. Reproduction
The third condition is the ability to replicate the behavior that the model has just demonstrated. This means that the observer has to be able to replicate the action, which could be a problem with a learner who is not ready developmentally to replicate the action.

4. Motivation
The final necessary ingredient for modeling to occur is motivation, learners must want to demonstrate what they have learned. Remember that since these four conditions vary among individuals, different people will reproduce the same behavior differently. Reinforcement and punishment play an important role in motivation.

Fig. 1.5 Social learning theory and its modeling process. This figure illustrates the key components of the modeling process in Social Learning Theory, including attention, retention, reproduction, and motivation. These elements are foundational to understanding the observational learning aspects emphasized in RCT. Reproduced with permission licensed under CC BY 4.0 (Schunk, 2012)

and modeling, SCLT projects environment/situation as the key feature that influence behavior and skills through observing, understanding, predicting and changing behavior. SCT suggests comprehensive interactionism between individual aspects, behavior, and environmental aspects. This model does not advocate equivalent weightages for all three attributes, and also, the effect is not necessarily observed immediately but may also take into effect in a prolonged period of time. SCT is grounded in the belief that individuals are unique in their aptitude to epitomize experiences, to foster anticipation about consequences for their actions, to learn through the actions of others, and to change their behavior through self-reflection and self-regulation (Bozack, 2011).

Research is also often associated with a lesser percentage of the learner population, as it encounters numerous learning responsibilities in accomplishing goals without guaranteeing the outcomes. It is not necessary that every research outcome is productive, which indeed can also negatively impact their motivation. This cyclic behavior aligns with Bandura's SCLT, as there is no distinct outcome at the end of a process. As in the case of developed countries, reports identify a huge shortcoming in the STEM (Science, Technology, Engineering and Mathematics) domain-based workforce, as individuals refrain from tasks that involve research and technical labor. STEM based tasks are categorically framed to involve higher order thinking and innovation, which demands a cache of menial tasks. The young learners in these countries tend to refrain themselves from "tough work" as they do not have the drive/motivation to take part in the action, as they are not subjected to difficulties that make their living conditions vulnerable. As necessity is the mother of invention, desires are the mother of motivation. Countries that have ample resources to sustain lack desires as the needs of their residents are always limited. As such developed countries are facing serious problems in motivating their younger generation with sustainability needs. The students are not subjected to challenging situations that either threaten their existence or cause disruption to their daily lives.

As such, to teach or train them, environments are structured, thereby simulating the environment with necessary. Hence, in the case of less motivated students, we need to structure a dynamic research environment challenging the students to take part in one or more research driven activities. This environment can be structured according to the demands from a specific educational tier, thereby adopting a constructivist approach to build a gradual array of learning experiences according to the levels, developing positive behavior -attitudes and competencies. When research learning is practiced as a conditioning environment, a naturally less or not motivated individual is expected to learn habitually through structured challenging dynamic environment. In this case, the constructivist approach can be adopted for a solid behavioral change that can guarantee a long-term effect. A less or not motivated learner can be subjected to one or more outcomes-based actions, which gradually instills the outcomes using a constructivist approach and complements each other. This observation is based on the 13 years of research-based assessment at different educational tiers—primary, preparatory and high school dealing with numerous less motivated students, being in a developed country. Similar structured and one of the most effective environments is the informal learning programs and research experience models as it positively enhances the likelihood to choose STEM careers and/or build research competencies (Sabirova & Zakirova, 2015; Swank & Lambie, 2016; Whalen & Shelley, 2010; Xu, 2013). This observation is closely aligned with Bandura's Social cognitive theory (SCT) whereby he clearly distinguishes his theory from other theories based on the emphasis he stresses on the significant role of cognition in human behavior. A research environment can engage the learners to develop their behavior, thereby modifying their attitudes and display different competencies, which intactly leads to the Research Cognitive learning Theory. Research experiences offer a highly cognitive learning environment as it practices and demands highly analytical and thinking based learning experience. It is a sustainable learning environment that features a research community, research learners, and their progressive development in terms of skill, attitude and knowledge. It establishes a dynamic learning environment,

1.3 Learning Models and Underlying Theories in Research Learning

whereby learners develop curiosity from their surroundings that include either the project parameters or scientist role models. This curiosity developed within the individual excites and develops an intrinsic motivation, which is therefore exhibited as a research behavior. Based on the principle of retention in SLT, learners upon a structured curiosity, can be subjected to extended period of analytical practices, thereby equipping them with the skills and motivation. Although, research experiences were highly impactful on the students who are motivated or possess a natural curiosity to drive themselves into research-based activities, they easily role model the researchers in the context and get motivated to exhibit positive behavior.

While detailing the impact of the environment, we may consider the different aspects of research environment that contribute to a dynamic execution, thereby mainly focusing on the research community and their actions. The research community as we address here, comprises of research project mentors, research assistants, lab technicians, and research peers. According to Bandura's SLT, the interaction between a research learner and research mentor is the key to the behavioral change in the student. Meanwhile SCT advocates on the interaction between the learner and all other community members also attribute to the change in the learner behavior, which leads to the concept of research based cognitive development. The research community hold a dynamic learning environment, as a learner individual acquires knowledge from all the other surrounding parties, as they exchange information, technical expertise and motivational dialogues. Gelso in 1993, proposed the theory of Research Training Environment (RTE) in the context of graduate programs in professional psychology, which also emphasizes on the positive impact of environment in ensuring scientific productivity, especially from the influence of faculty (Gelso, 1993). Gelso states that "The scientific behavior and attitudes of the faculty are probably the most fundamentally important research-enhancing (or retarding, if negative) ingredient in the overall RTE". Meanwhile, we believe that irrespective of the research disciplines or student educational tiers, research environment plays a vital role in molding the learner research behavior. The environment promotes a positive outlook on the learners as they get subjected to learner methods that intrigue them, motivate them to place themselves under action, improvise their actions in a productive way and gradually motivate them to act independently. This motivation leads them to develop a positive attitude towards research and thereby play the role of a problem solver or an innovator to solve specific solutions. The key feature of subjecting learners into similar environments is the reciprocity that is maintained among the research community. All the classes of the research community experience learning with the interactions that lead to new profound knowledge, skill development or cognitive development thereby framing a dynamic learning environment. As the interactionism is taking place in the limits of a research environment, we propose that SCT can be extended to the research cognitive theory (RCT). RCT postulates that intellectual learning occurs in a dynamic research environment and reciprocal interaction of the individual, environment, and behavior. The distinctive feature of RCT is the consequence of dynamic research environment influence and its emphasis on intrinsic intellectual reinforcement. Learners enhance their cognitive behavior especially in intellectual development, both intrinsic and extrinsic as well as tacit knowledge as they are subjected to the environment enclosed by research community. The intellectual development also extends towards augmenting their research attitudes specifically research self-efficacy and research interest as well as fostering different research skills validated by RSD framework. This proposal is based on the different empirical studies that have been conducted world-wide as well as from our own studies that signifies the impact of different research environment on learner's intellectual as well as cognitive behavior.

In the process, RCT also consolidates the principle in which individuals acquire and maintain their intellectual behavior in a research environment, while also considering the social environment in which individuals perform the behavior. As continuous interactions are made in a dynamic environment like research experiences as social connection is being made within the research community, RCT advocates the existence of intellectual behavioral action occurrence. According to RCT, the dynamic research experiences will therefore influence reinforcements, prospects, and beliefs, of the learners, which explains the learning behavioral evolution of a learner, engaged in an intellectual learning. As we break down the theory, the first part describes the influence of individual research practices on the development of intrinsic motivation, i.e. the motivation to pursue/perform research practices and influential factors on the consequential individual intellectual behaviors. And the second part corresponds to the continuous effect on the evolving intellectual behavior as a learner matures into an independent researcher, aligning to the cyclic effect of the social interactions by the learner individual as posited by Bandura's SCT. RCT provides opportunities for intellectual support through instilling expectations, self-efficacy, and using research learning and other reinforcements to achieve behavior change. RCT also considers a person's past experiences, which factor into whether behavioral action will occur. These past experiences influence reinforcements, expectations, and expectancies, all which shape whether a person will engage in a specific behavior and the reasons why a person engages in that behavior. Fig. 1.6 shows the representation of the proposed theory.

The identified key components of the RCT based on the different theories that are related to individual behavior change and evolve from the continuous social interactions are given in Appendix B. In the coming chapters, we will be discussing how RCT is proposed as the theoretical framework for different research learning practices, thereafter, detailing the different aspects of RCT under different empirical research settings.

1.4 Chapter Summary

In summary, this chapter introduces the concept of Research Learning (RL) and explores its impact on learner development across physical, cognitive, and psychological dimensions. It begins by defining research as a systematic process aimed at discovering solutions or generating new ideas through inquiry and investigation. The chapter discusses how engaging in research fosters curiosity, critical thinking,

1.4 Chapter Summary

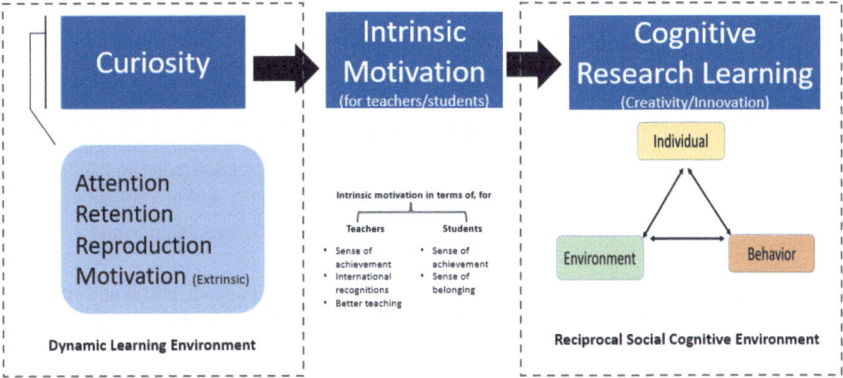

Fig. 1.6 Representation of the proposed research cognitive theory. This figure illustrates the RCT framework, emphasizing the progression from curiosity to intrinsic motivation and cognitive research learning. It integrates social cognitive theory to highlight reciprocal interactions among individuals, behaviors, and their environment. Key components include self-efficacy, behavioral capability, expectations, self-control, observational learning, and reinforcements, fostering creativity and innovation within a dynamic learning environment. Figure by authors

problem-solving, and creativity, which are key aspects of intellectual and psychosocial maturation. Through RL, students gain essential research skills, including data collection, analysis, and the ability to draw meaningful conclusions, all of which contribute to the development of knowledge, attitudes, and skills.

The chapter also introduces two main approaches to research learning: Learning through Independent Research and Learning through Integrated/Embedded Research. It highlights how each method contributes to the development of different learner competencies. Furthermore, the chapter outlines the essential steps of the research process—identifying key questions, gathering data, analysis, and disseminating findings—and examines how these processes support the physical, cognitive, and psychological readiness of learners. The chapter emphasizes the role of research in cultivating knowledge, enhancing attitudes, and fostering cognitive development, which are crucial for success in the twenty-first century.

In addition, the chapter delves into the relationship between research learning and existing educational theories, such as Social Learning Theory (SLT) and Social Cognitive Theory (SCT), and how these frameworks provide a foundation for understanding the dynamic interaction between learners, their environment, and the behaviors they engage in during the research process. This section sets the stage for subsequent discussions on how research-based learning approaches can be integrated into educational practices to improve learner outcomes across various educational levels.

Glossary

Term	Definition
Research Learning (RL)	The process of acquiring knowledge and skills through systematic inquiry and investigation
Curiosity	An intrinsic desire to explore, inquire, and understand
Critical Thinking	The ability to analyze, evaluate, and synthesize information to form logical conclusions or solve problems
Problem-Solving	A cognitive process of identifying solutions to complex or unfamiliar issues
Cognitive Development	The maturation of mental processes, including critical thinking, creativity, and problem-solving
Self-Efficacy	An individual's belief in their ability to perform tasks or achieve goals
Social Learning Theory (SLT)	A theory positing that learning occurs through observing, modeling, and interacting with others
Social Cognitive Theory (SCT)	A framework emphasizing the interplay between personal factors, behaviors, and environmental influences
Research Attitude	A learner's outlook or disposition towards conducting research, influenced by interest and aspirations
21st-Century Skills	Competencies like critical thinking, creativity, collaboration, communication, and adaptability essential for success
Inquiry-Based Learning (IBL)	A pedagogical approach where students learn by engaging in structured questioning and problem-solving
Embedded Research Learning	Integrating research practices into the curriculum to promote interdisciplinary learning and collaboration
Tacit Knowledge	Unrecorded, experiential knowledge gained through practice and experience
Constructivist Approach	A learning philosophy emphasizing the active role of learners in constructing knowledge through experiences
Research Skill Development Framework (RSD)	A structured model for fostering research skills, highlighting autonomy and inquiry-based learning
Course-Based Undergraduate Research Experiences (CUREs)	A pedagogical model involving students in structured research projects, promoting discovery and collaboration

(continued)

(continued)

Term	Definition
Dynamic Research Environment	An interactive setting fostering reciprocal interactions between learners and mentors for cognitive growth
Behavioral Capability	An individual's ability to understand and execute a specific behavior or task
Intrinsic Motivation	Internal drive to engage in tasks or behaviors out of personal interest or satisfaction
Observational Learning	Acquiring skills or behaviors by observing and imitating others
Expectancies	The value placed on outcomes or goals as a motivator for behavior
Reinforcements	Incentives or rewards that encourage specific behaviors
Interdisciplinary Research	An approach integrating methods and perspectives from multiple disciplines to address complex problems
Apprenticeship Model	A traditional learning approach where learners gain skills through close mentorship and observation of experts
Research Cognitive Theory (RCT)	A framework linking research activities to cognitive, social, and behavioral development in research environments

References

Adedokun, O. A., & Burgess, W. D. (2011). Uncovering students' preconceptions of undergraduate research experiences. *Journal of STEM Education: Innovations and research, 12*(5).

Adedokun, O. A., Zhang, D., Parker, L. C., Bessenbacher, A., Childress, A., & Burgess, W. D. (2012). Understanding how undergraduate research experiences influence student aspirations for research careers and graduate education. *Journal of College Science Teaching, 42*(1), 82.

Al-Thani, N., Bhadra, J., Siby, N., Elhawary, E., & Saad, A. (2020). Innovative tool to educate high school students through research based learning.

Al-Thani, N. J., Saad, A., Siby, N., Bhadra, J., & Ahmad, Z. (2022). The role of multidisciplinary chemistry informal research programs in building research competencies and attitudes. *Journal of Chemical Education, 99*(5), 1957–1970.

Albareda-Tiana, S., Vidal-Raméntol, S., Pujol-Valls, M., & Fernández-Morilla, M. (2018). Holistic approaches to develop sustainability and research competencies in pre-service teacher training. *Sustainability, 10*(10), 3698. https://www.mdpi.com/2071-1050/10/10/3698

Apps, J. W. (1972). Toward a broader definition of research. *Adult Education, 23*(1), 59–64.

Auchincloss, L. C., Laursen, S. L., Branchaw, J. L., Eagan, K., Graham, M., Hanauer, D. I., Lawrie, G., McLinn, C. M., Pelaez, N., & Rowland, S. (2014). Assessment of course-based undergraduate research experiences: A meeting report. *CBE—Life Sciences Education, 13*(1), 29–40.

Bain, R. (1928). An attitude on attitude research. *American Journal of Sociology, 33*(6), 940–957.

Bandura, A. (1971). Vicarious and self-reinforcement processes. *The Nature of Reinforcement,* 228278.
Bandura, A. J. T. H. P. R. (2002). 6 Social foundations of thought and action. 94.
Barab, S. A., & Hay, K. E. (2001). Doing science at the elbows of experts: Issues related to the science apprenticeship camp. *Journal of Research in Science Teaching, 38*(1), 70–102.
Barrow, L. H. (2006). A brief history of inquiry: From Dewey to standards. *Journal of Science Teacher Education, 17*(3), 265–278.
Boyer, E. L. (1990). *Scholarship reconsidered: Priorities of the professoriate.* ERIC.
Bozack, A. (2011). Social cognitive learning theory. In S. Goldstein & J. A. Naglieri (Eds.), *Encyclopedia of child behavior and development* (pp. 1392–1394). Springer US. https://doi.org/10.1007/978-0-387-79061-9_2715
Brown, J. S., Collins, A., & Duguid, P. (1989). Situated cognition and the culture of learning. *18*(1), 32–42.
Burgin, S. R., & Sadler, T. D. (2016). Learning nature of science concepts through a research apprenticeship program: A comparative study of three approaches. *Journal of Research in Science Teaching, 53*(1), 31–59.
Camacho, M., Valcke, M., & Chiluiza, K. (2017). Research based learning in higher education: A review of literature. In *INTED2017 Proceedings* (pp. 4188–4197).
Christophorou, L., & Hunter, S. (1984). From basic research to application. *Electron-Molecule Interactions and Their Applications, 2*(2), 318.
Cunliffe, A. L. (2020). Reflexivity in teaching and researching organizational studies. *Revista de Administração de Empresas, 60,* 64–69.
Dewey, J. (1997). Experience and education. *The Educational Forum, 1938–8098, 50*(3), 241–252. https://www.concrete.org/students/studentcompetitions/frcbowlingballcompetition.aspx#:~:text=The%20objective%20of%20this%20competition,in%20engineering%20design%20and%20analysis
Etzkowitz, H. (2003). Research groups as 'quasi-firms': The invention of the entrepreneurial university. *Research Policy, 32*(1), 109–121.
Gelso, C. J. (1993). On the making of a scientist-practitioner: A theory of research training in professional psychology. *Professional Psychology: Research and Practice, 24*(4), 468–476. https://doi.org/10.1037/0735-7028.24.4.468
Ghanem, E., Long, S. R., Rodenbusch, S. E., Shear, R. I., Beckham, J. T., Procko, K., DePue, L., Stevenson, K. J., Robertus, J. D., Martin, S., Holliday, B., Jones, R. A., Anslyn, E. V., & Simmons, S. L. (2018, February 13). Teaching through research: Alignment of core chemistry competencies and skills within a multidisciplinary research framework. *Journal of Chemical Education, 95*(2), 248–258. https://doi.org/10.1021/acs.jchemed.7b00294
Goddard, A. (1998). http://www.timeshighereducation.co.uk/news/facing-up-to-market-forces/109862.article
Guile, D., & Young, M. (1998). Apprenticeship as a conceptual basis for a social theory of learning. *Journal of Vocational Education & Training, 50*(2), 173–193.
Healey, M., & Jenkins, A. (2009). *Developing undergraduate research and inquiry.* Higher Education Academy York.
Hmelo-Silver, C. E., Duncan, R. G., & Chinn, C. A. (2007). Scaffolding and achievement in problem-based and inquiry learning: A response to Kirschner, Sweller, and. *Educational Psychologist, 42*(2), 99–107.
Holme, T. A. (1994). Providing motivation for the general chemistry course through early introduction of current research topics. *Journal of Chemical Education, 71*(11), 919.
Hunter, A.-B., Laursen, S. L., & Seymour, E. (2007). Becoming a scientist: The role of undergraduate research in students' cognitive, personal, and professional development. *Science education, 91*(1), 36–74. https://doi.org/10.1002/sce.20173
Jones, M. T., Barlow, A. E., & Villarejo, M. (2010). Importance of undergraduate research for minority persistence and achievement in biology. *The Journal of Higher Education, 81*(1), 82–115.

References

Kittur, H., Shaw, L., & Herrera, W. (2017). A new model for a multi-disciplinary engineering summer research program for high school seniors: Program overview, effectiveness, and outcomes. *Journal of STEM Education, 18*(4).

Knight, R.-A., & Botting, N. (2016). Organising undergraduate research projects: Student-led and academic-led models. *Journal of Applied Research in Higher Education, 8*(4), 455–468. https://doi.org/10.1108/JARHE-07-2015-0054

Kubisch, S., Parth, S., Deisenrieder, V., Oberauer, K., Stötter, J., & Keller, L. (2021). From transdisciplinary research to transdisciplinary education—The role of schools in contributing to community well-being and sustainable development. *Sustainability, 13*(1), 306.

Laursen, S., Hunter, A.-B., Seymour, E., Thiry, H., & Melton, G. (2010). *Undergraduate research in the sciences: Engaging students in real science*. Wiley.

Lave, J., & Wenger, E. (1991). *Situated learning: Legitimate peripheral participation*. Cambridge University Press.

Lazonder, A. W., & Harmsen, R. (2016). Meta-analysis of inquiry-based learning: Effects of guidance. *Review of Educational Research, 86*(3), 681–718.

Lent, R. W., Brown, S. D., & Hackett, G. (1994). Toward a unifying social cognitive theory of career and academic interest, choice, and performance. *Journal of Vocational Behavior, 45*(1), 79–122.

Lent, R. W., Brown, S. D., & Hackett, G. (2000). Contextual supports and barriers to career choice: A social cognitive analysis. *Journal of Counseling Psychology, 47*(1), 36.

Lent, R. W., Singley, D., Sheu, H.-B., Gainor, K. A., Brenner, B. R., Treistman, D., & Ades, L. (2005). Social cognitive predictors of domain and life satisfaction: Exploring the theoretical precursors of subjective well-being. *Journal of Counseling Psychology, 52*(3), 429.

Leontovich, A. (2003). Projecting research activity of pupils. In *Moscow, Institute of Pedagogical Innovations of Russian Science Academy dissertation*, 142.

MacIntosh, R., Beech, N., Antonacopoulou, E., & Sims, D. (2012). Practising and knowing management: A dialogic perspective. *Management Learning, 43*(4), 373–383. https://doi.org/10.1177/1350507612452521

McLaughlin, J. S., Favre, D. E., Weinstein, S. E., & Goedhart, C. M. (2017). The impact of a four-step laboratory pedagogical framework on biology students' perceptions of laboratory skills, knowledge, and interest in research. *Journal of College Science Teaching, 47*(1).

McMiller, T., Lee, T., Saroop, R., Green, T., & Johnson, C. M. (2006). Middle/high school students in the research laboratory: A summer internship program emphasizing the interdisciplinary nature of biology. *Biochemistry and Molecular Biology Education, 34*(2), 88–93. https://doi.org/10.1002/bmb.2006.49403402088

Meerah, T. S. M., & Arsad, N. M. (2010). Developing research skills at secondary school. *Procedia-Social and Behavioral Sciences, 9*, 512–516.

Mellander, E., & Svärdh, J. (2018). Inquiry-based learning put to the test: Medium-term effects of a science and technology for children programme. *Review of Education, 6*(2), 103–141.

Michael, O., Crowley, S., Eigenbrode, S. D., & Wulfhorst, J. (2013). *Enhancing communication & collaboration in interdisciplinary research*. Sage Publications.

Puerta, M. L. S., Valerio, A., & Bernal, M. G. (2016). Taking stock of programs to develop socioemotional skills: A systematic review of program evidence.

Ruth, A., Brewis, A., & SturtzSreetharan, C. (2023, October 3). Effectiveness of social science research opportunities: A study of course-based undergraduate research experiences (CUREs). *Teaching in Higher Education, 28*(7), 1484–1502. https://doi.org/10.1080/13562517.2021.1903853

Sabirova, E. G., & Zakirova, V. G. (2015). Formation of pupils' research skills in informational and educational environment of elementary school. *Procedia-Social and Behavioral Sciences, 191*, 1139–1142.

Sadler, T. D., Burgin, S., McKinney, L., & Ponjuan, L. (2010). Learning science through research apprenticeships: A critical review of the literature. *Journal of Research in Science Teaching: The*

Official Journal of the National Association for Research in Science Teaching, 47(3), 235–256. https://doi.org/10.1002/tea.20326

Schunk, D. H. (2012). *Learning theories an educational perspective.* Pearson Education, Inc.

Swank, J. M., & Lambie, G. W. (2016). Development of the research competencies scale. *49*(2), 91–108. https://doi.org/10.1177/0748175615625749

Vereijken, M. W., van der Rijst, R. M., van Driel, J. H., & Dekker, F. W. (2018). Student learning outcomes, perceptions and beliefs in the context of strengthening research integration into the first year of medical school. *Advances in Health Sciences Education, 23,* 371–385.

Whalen, D. F., & Shelley, M. C. (2010). Academic success for STEM and non-STEM majors. *Journal of STEM Education: Innovations and research, 11*(1).

Willison, J., & O'Regan, K. (2007). Commonly known, commonly not known, totally unknown: A framework for students becoming researchers. *Higher Education Research & Development, 26*(4), 393–409.

Xu, Y. J. (2013). Career outcomes of STEM and non-STEM college graduates: Persistence in majored-field and influential factors in career choices. *Research in Higher Education, 54*(3), 349–382.

Open Access This chapter is licensed under the terms of the Creative Commons Attribution 4.0 International License (http://creativecommons.org/licenses/by/4.0/), which permits use, sharing, adaptation, distribution and reproduction in any medium or format, as long as you give appropriate credit to the original author(s) and the source, provide a link to the Creative Commons license and indicate if changes were made.

The images or other third party material in this chapter are included in the chapter's Creative Commons license, unless indicated otherwise in a credit line to the material. If material is not included in the chapter's Creative Commons license and your intended use is not permitted by statutory regulation or exceeds the permitted use, you will need to obtain permission directly from the copyright holder.

Chapter 2
The Scope of Problem-Based Learning and Integrated Research Education for Primary Learners

Abstract This Chapter 2 examines the significant role of problem-based learning (PBL) and integrated research education in shaping cognitive development and educational outcomes for primary learners. The chapter begins by detailing how fostering curiosity through research-driven inquiry is essential for intellectual growth and cognitive skill enhancement. It highlights the dynamic relationship between curiosity and Inquiry-Based Learning (IBL), emphasizing how curiosity drives investigative behavior and knowledge acquisition. Additionally, it explores the concept of epistemic curiosity and its impact on student motivation and learning. The chapter further explores the integration of scientific inquiry with problem-solving skills, drawing on recent research to illustrate how PBL can enhance critical thinking, interpersonal abilities, and collaborative skills. It examines the balance between direct instruction and open experimentation, presenting studies that evaluate the effectiveness of various instructional methods in developing problem-solving expertise. Emphasis is placed on the role of metacognition in improving problem-solving abilities and the necessity of structured learning environments that support creative problem-solving and metacognitive strategies. Additionally, Chapter 2 investigates the transformative influence of digital technology on research and problem-based learning. It reviews recent advancements in digital tools and resources, highlighting their role in enhancing student engagement, motivation, and inquiry skills. The chapter discusses technology-enhanced approaches, such as Technology-Enhanced Problem-Based Learning Activities (TEPLA) and Technology-Based Inquiry Approaches (TBIA), and their impact on educational practices and learning outcomes. It also addresses challenges related to integrating technology in educational contexts, particularly in developing regions, and presents innovative solutions like the Stanford Mobile Inquiry-Based Learning Environment (SMILE) and digital applications designed to foster inquiry and problem-solving skills. Overall, Chapter 2 provides a comprehensive overview of how PBL and integrated research education, supported by technological advancements, contribute to the development of critical cognitive skills in primary education. It underscores the importance of creating dynamic, technology-enabled learning environments that foster curiosity, problem-solving, and scientific inquiry.

© The Author(s) 2025
N. J. Al-Thani and Z. Ahmad, *Teaching and Learning with Research Cognitive Theory*, SpringerBriefs in Education, https://doi.org/10.1007/978-3-031-87544-1_2

Keywords Problem-Based Learning (PBL) · Scientific Inquiry · Curiosity-Driven Learning · Digital Technology in Education · Research-Driven Inquiry

2.1 Fostering Curiosity Through Research-Driven Inquiry

Curiosity is a fundamental aspect of human nature that drives individuals to seek understanding and meaning in the world. As individuals involve in the procedure of exploring information, they require the mindset which allows for questioning and inquiry (Buch & Wolff, 2000) and plays a significant role in the intellectual growth of learners. This approach to learning involves both reasoned and instinctual learning, allowing students to move effectively between practical experiences and paradigms of reality. Within this dialectical process, curiosity manifests more organically, prompting students to acknowledge gaps in their knowledge and compelling them to actively pursue means to address these gaps. As students engage in this process of research-driven inquiry, their curiosity can be stoked to alert them to potential interest development, thus fueling the growth of their interest in the subject matter. Research addressing curiosity emphasizes its significance in distinguishing it from other characteristics like interest and wonder, highlighting its integral role in the educational journey of students (Oudeyer et al., 2016).

Incorporating teaching and learning theories, we can see that the role of curiosity extends beyond mere interest or inquisitiveness. It involves the ability to reject absolute knowledge and embrace a dynamic approach to knowledge acquisition. Students need to adeptly maneuver between tangible real-life encounters and theoretical models of the world. This dialectic process of learning involves both rational and intuitive aspects, allowing for a more organic flow of curiosity (Abd-El-Khalick et al., 2004). By recognizing the importance of curiosity and inquiry learning, educators can create an environment that nurtures intellectual development and fosters a deeper understanding of learning principles. Through this approach, students are encouraged to explore, question, and critically analyze, ultimately contributing to their overall growth and success in the field of engineering.

Curiosity drives to acquiring knowledge, as researches depict an affirmative relation within emotion handling, curiosity, reflection (Lauriola et al., 2015), effective learning strategies (Muis et al., 2015) and learning outcomes (Trevors et al., 2017; Zion & Sadeh, 2007). Recent scientific research offers a conceptual explanation in terms of the connection within curiosity and Inquiry-Based Learning (IBL). It demonstrates unpredictability as a vital component in describing IBL environment and also as a key element in learner's inclination towards curiosity. In the realm of educational approaches and guidelines, the significant factor influencing learner's engagement in IBL is curiosity (Glogger-Frey et al., 2015; Jirout & Klahr, 2012; Klahr et al., 2011). In the context of primary education, research driven learning is normally addressed as IBL and we will be hereafter disserting RL with respect to IBL. As per the comprehensive review of scholarly articles, learner's curiosity serves as a margin for seeking the unknown which results in an investigative behavior. The Information-Gap Decision

2.1 Fostering Curiosity Through Research-Driven Inquiry

Theory by Loewenstein (1994) confers to the fact that the incentive to resolve an issue arises due to the lack of knowledge, often described as experiencing an information gap (Arnone et al., 1994; Zion & Sadeh, 2007). A study in science education demonstrated that engaging in inventive activities enhances learner's curiosity, aligning to the inquiry-based educational setting (Glogger-Frey et al., 2015). However, there are questions among researchers whether IBL impacts young learners with curiosity at its early stages. Arnone and his research team (1994) explored this inquiry within the realm of art education (Arnone et al., 1994). They conducted a study involving young learners engaging in tech-dependent educational setting showcasing artistic video presentations. The researchers analyzed conditions with varying levels of structure (e.g., advisement to pause and reflect) among learners categorized based on different levels of curiosity. The study revealed that highly curious learners gained more knowledge of art principles and realities through research-driven learning compared to their less curious counterparts. However, no significant effects were observed for conditions or connections between curiosity and innate ability. The scholars attributed these observations from the typical learning practices to distinctiveness of the educational setting, which could have reduced disparities among circumstances. This study is grounded under the principles of RCT, whereby they discovered that the design of the surroundings favorably influenced the depth of learner's inquiry, particularly in the case of those with lower intelligence levels. An increasing repository of information supports incorporating research-driven methods into scientific discipline. Undoubtedly, learners exhibit greater motivation and interest in learning when they actively engage as part of the instructional journey. By examining intriguing issues stimulating creative reasoning and fostering curiosity, the learners contribute actively to reaching mutually agreed-upon conclusions (Gillies et al., 2012).

When it comes to understanding the role of building curiosity in learners from the social sciences context, Genesee (1994) claims that comprehending the material serves as a powerful incentive to carry information of personal interest, particularly in case of language students. (Nichols et al., 2017). By fostering curiosity, posing inquiries, and actively pursuing answers, language learners enhance their grasp of subjects and refine their language abilities concurrently. More specifically, learners acquire tacit knowledge as they engage with the target language, absorbing its patterns and structures without deliberate focus on acquisition. Through IBL, learners are active during the knowledge acquisition process, they encourage the exploration of diverse thought-provoking queries, foster self-reliant learning, instill a sense of responsibility for acquiring knowledge, and promote a lifelong commitment to seeking and gaining information (Wu et al., 2015). IBL offers language learners valuable experiences by fostering creativity, encouraging reflection, promoting discovery, and enhancing cognitive skills. Beyond these benefits, IBL ensures that learners become active knowledge inquirers rather than passive receivers of information. This valuable experience plays a crucial role in facilitating future self-regulated learning and eventual success.

Epistemic curiosity involves a keen interest in acquiring novel intellectual knowledge and is recognized for motivating intricate exploratory actions (Post & van der

Molen, 2021). As per Theories of Attitudes, scholars considered cognitive understanding as a factor that can thrive solely on learning environments where students recognize the cognitive value, enjoyment, recognition and the potential for becoming learners with a curious mindset (Post & van der Molen, 2018). Collectively, these perceptions—intellectual, emotional, conventional and regulatory—can influence engaging or abstaining from certain behaviors. While attitudes typically remain consistent over time, interventions like deliberate reflection and discussion activities that create an inquisitive environment will have the potential to enhance them. Scholars have conceptualized the components of students' attitudes towards cognitive understanding into five categories based upon the Planned Behavior Theory, which might lead to students' cognitive understanding about educational environments, personal preferences, public significance, concern over negative opinion from peers and lastly self-efficacy. Diverse interventions and exercises which gave rise to the evolution of epistemic curiosity are detailed below.

- Acting as a mentor to students for applying curiosity to delve into new topics, whether through the formulation of follow-up inquiries or contemplation of alternative concepts.
- Motivating students by sharing impactful statements of prominent scholars and engineers featured in the media, highlighting the impact by curious people in shaping society.
- It is essential that students welcome and encourage mutual curiosity-driven thoughts, concerns and perspectives related to the context before embarking in a collaborative investigation.
- Upon completion of a project, encourage students to reflect on any instances of curiosity-driven behavior exhibited by their peers that they found inspiring and would like to incorporate into their own learning.
- Recognizing students who ask insightful follow-up questions during lesson exploration, for example, by presenting tiny gifts or showcasing the questions in the classroom.

2.2 What is Scientific Inquiry?

Research-driven education is a learner-focused, hands-on learning strategy emphasizing inquiry or research. It involves presenting students with a series of questions or tasks, prompting them to solve and comprehend them. This method challenges students to delve deeply into course material, fostering a thorough understanding analogous to the literature review process while performing research. IBL promotes increased activity and autonomy in learners as they acquire knowledge, focusing on addressing students' needs and interests. As while performing research, instructors do not impart all information precisely. Alternatively, they motivate young students to explore information and formulate underlying rules through a diverse set of instances and their counterparts. The investigation process captures the students' interest and active engagement due to the alignment of topics with their needs and

2.2 What is Scientific Inquiry?

interests (Wilson & Murdoch, 2016). Hence, experimenting through research-driven learning empowers students to experiment, explore, pose questions, engage in critical thinking, reflect on their progress, and become mindful of their learning preferences and pace. Science activities driving inquiry involves learners in hands on activities. Additionally, they receive resources to aid their grasp of field expertise through involvement in scientific investigation and research methodologies such as thesis formation, conducting experiments and evaluating validation. It offers a dual benefit: learners can cultivate comprehension and expertise regarding observed scientific phenomena in the real world, while also gaining insight into executing scientific inquiry steps akin to scientists. These two facets are interconnected because students cannot engage in inquiry effectively unless they possess the necessary skills and conversely, proficiency in a specific domain is essential in investigative abilities. Studies in research-driven education underscores the crucial requirement for helping learners overcome challenges associated with tasks like data driven conclusions. Assistance for inquiry can take various forms, including simulations, accompanying software, educators, or other educational resources. All these tools form an active environment whereby student-centered approach is being cultivated while performing a research-based activity like inquiry. Currently, a significant portion of studies in research driven education are primarily centered to mobile technology in learning science utilizing data-driven or theory driven research methods. It indicates that the learners are involved in processing their ideas or thesis to investigate identified scenarios or circumstances. Conversely, backward reasoning centers around generating hypotheses related to observed phenomena.

A crucial element of scientific investigation is its ability to connect information with the procedural aspects (Cremin et al., 2018). When students participate in scientific inquiry, they not only enhance their grasp of scientific concepts but also develop a deeper understanding of the scientific process. Engaging in practical activities and investigations holds a promise of improving their thinking skills like meta-awareness and reasoning abilities. To sum up, these tasks elevate a student's grasp of knowledge and concepts, intellectual and practical proficiencies as well as insights into the essence of scientific education. Furthermore, they contribute to fostering students' motivation and fostering positive attitudes towards science (Areepattamannil, 2012). Indeed, researchers advocate that young learners thrive academically within a learner-focused, constructivist learning setting that promotes interactive, inductive, and collaborative knowledge construction (Kaberman & Dori, 2009; Ozkal et al., 2009). The focus on the importance of learner settings also grounds our theory, that postulates on the development of intellectual learning in learners from a dynamic environment. These research findings indicate that ultimately, the implementation of inquiry driven activities in primary education significantly contributes to their engagement in science and development of metacognitive skills.

We could decipher the large pool of literature that incited about meaningfulness of scientific exploration and its conceptualization from two dimensions, specifically, the type of teaching interventions that the learner engages in and the impact of teacher instruction (Akuma & Callaghan, 2019; Dobber et al., 2017; Rönnebeck et al., 2016; Shymansky et al., 2003). It is vital to analyze students' learning behavior on different inquiry-based activities—structured and guided, both classrooms based as well as part of a scientific laboratory through guidance from scholars and educators. As for the case of primary students, it applies to only classroom context, it is reasonable that it can be related to the actions in the research context as in the case of higher stages of education. From the research of eminent scholars, we could also infer the effect of learning environments with research or inquiry driven learning on the students' learning behavior (Lin et al., 2009). This was similar to the case of high school learners, wherein McElhany and Linn put learners 'in formulating informative activities' and 'in elucidating mechanisms' of a particular circumstances (McElhaney & Linn, 2011). While learners in earlier research carried out practical experiential learning in research laboratory, learners from later study experimented in an online environment. Hence, according to inferences from a study (Furtak et al., 2012)m, it seems inevitable not to converge solely on the conceptual context of inquiry, but also to understand and apply the different processes involved in engaging students in inquiry that has a causal effect on student learning behavior.

While discussing the perspectives of designing settings in a classroom inquiry driven learning context, it is equally important to realize the effect of the environment on the inquiry process and student learning development. The inquiry driven approach represents one of the most realistic teaching approaches in the elementary stages of education, aligning seamlessly with the demands of the 21st century. It cultivates student interest and establishes an interactive learning setting that strongly encourages discovery, reflection, and creative learning, as supported by the previous research, thereby advocating the teaching and learning through RCT (Nichols et al., 2017). The learners are deeply engraved in active participation, thereby enhancing their knowledge both implicit and explicit, resulting in developing responsibility for their quest for novel knowledge. Resultantly, teachers have a passive role in feeding students with restricted contextual knowledge rather than the learners open their investigation, leading to boundless discoveries. As the stress on teaching converges on exploration, learners don the role of self-regulated learning with autonomy and self-interest. The design of the activity determines the learner's deep interest in the intellectual learning process and inspires the consequent actions that cultivate their cognition. They display keen willingness to develop their knowledge under the present conditions, which is crucially significant for the effective learning outcomes.

Systematic inquiry encompasses the intricate intellectual and introspective abilities which require continuous practice as well as refinement over time. In a comprehensive sense, it encompasses the competencies, information, and methodologies related to investigation, experimentation, critical assessment of evidence, and drawing inferences, all contributing to the development of a scientific comprehension (Klahr et al., 2011). Researchers believe primary years in a child's learning period is crucial to developing scientific thinking (Harlen, 2000; Osborne et al., 2003), which indeed lay out the base for determining a child's success and failure to an extent. Based on this conviction, numerous nations have incorporated the acquisition of fundamental scientific reasoning skills and practices into their primary school syllabus (Bybee, 2014). Within this set of dispositions and practices, fostering the

2.2 What is Scientific Inquiry?

capacity to strategize, execute, assess, and scrutinize experiments stands as a significant objective in global science education, especially research being one of the most recognized outcomes from science learning. Experimentation is one of the most pivotal techniques for acquiring a profound perception of scientific thinking and exploratory endeavors. In general, an experiment is characterized as a method used to test one or more hypotheses in the context of a specific phenomenon by testing and observing many variables. The research framework refers to the systematic structure of research, encompassing in logical structure for empirical procedures, specifically focusing on its planning and analysis. Learners, while grasping the experimental process, think in diverse ways to execute it systematically, thereby enhancing their scientific thinking capacity.

The research methodology skill outlays the list of minor abilities that involve understanding a research question that depicts a research problem, hypothesis construction, estimating experimental pre-requisites, determining and defining variables for testing, defining conditions to quantify, measure and compare findings, drawing out inferences and predicting the possible outcomes. However, these skills also fall under the category of research skills as defined under the RSD and hence, we may engage discussion on research skills to experimental skills. Previous research, however, leads to the conclusion that development of sub experimental skills in primary students is not an easy feat. Previous research implied that only 35% of 9-year old participants have the ability to find inaccuracies in methods while solving problems based on motion and force while another study, states that only 11% of grade 6 learners have the ability to emerge with inferences on reasons for environmental calamities like seismic activity despite attending interventions prior to foster that skill (Chen & Klahr, 1999; Dean Jr & Kuhn, 2007). Furthermore, learners wit a high level of advancement in scientific subjects exhibited persistent misconceptions in experimental design. In a study from Argentina that was carried out on 3900 learners from primary schools, for understanding the comparison in heat conductivity of different materials, only 9% of 6th graders designed a valid experiment (Di Mauro & Furman, 2016; Furman, 2012). In early stages of learner development, fostering scientific skills requires ample time and effort in effectively improving the scientific skills. However, IBL approaches have ensured to combat the limitations as perceived in the previous research in enhancing the scientific thinking skills (Di Mauro & Furman, 2016). This study led to the examination of diverse teaching strategies that improved the research framework of learners from grade 4 in Argentina (Di Mauro & Furman, 2016). Performance of the learners in developing important trials was assessed pre and post an intervention for eight weeks comparing to a reference group, and the continuity of the subsequent intervention later for eight consecutive months. Studies implicate that the enhancement in students' proficiency with the inquiry-based sequence is reflected in improved experimental design skills and sustained learning. Following the intervention, students successfully made valid comparisons, suggested relevant designs, and identified variables that needed to be kept constant. Conversely, those in the control group demonstrated no progress and persisted in solving problems based on pre-existing beliefs. To summarize, this study provides proof that the introduction of research-driven modules, incorporating issues in everyday multidisciplinary contexts, and combining self-directed learning activities under the guidance of mentors to enhance development of intellectual skills in authentic educational settings. This study clearly demonstrates the evolution of RCT, wherein an interactive learning environment through inquiry-based sequence integrated with the teacher/mentor's guided instructional approach that incites and excites the learners, holds the key to developing cognition and learning in students.

Reports on the different interventions indicate effectiveness in improving primary learners' cross—domain experimental skills (Ergül et al., 2011; Klahr & Nigam, 2004). Furthermore, they all recognize the importance of simplifying the cognitive and the complexity of concepts in the context in prioritizing advancement in skills related to science, such as designing an experimental framework. Although limited research has delved into educational interventions fostering comprehensive development of experimental skills, Di Mauro and Furman proposed integrating guided teaching and hands-on activities, led closely by teachers, to yield more favorable outcomes on both academic progress and their enduring impact (Di Mauro & Furman, 2016). Aligning to their recommendations, a study was performed in Turkey primary school advocated on the effectiveness of IBL activities in enhancing the primary school students' performance as of when compared to those receiving traditional education (Ergül et al., 2011). The quasi-experimental study was performed on grade 4, grade 5 and grade 6 students making a total strength of 144 wherein they collaborated with hands-on experiments to find solutions for the scientific problems, under the guidance of teachers through group discussions and direct instructions. Cross domain activities from physics, chemistry and biology resulted in a group efficiently demonstrating best outcomes than the other part based on their experimental skills. This study also pinpoints the emergence of principles of RCT, wherein learning environment and social interference (teacher guidance and peer discussion) play a significant role in the bolstering of student skills. Another study grounded by RCT also introduces the effect of an innovative inquiry based teaching intervention, the Biomind curriculum, for encouraging learners in adapting to the dynamic scientific procedure (Zion & Sadeh, 2007). It fosters student participation in self-guided exploration, personal drive, and collaborative teamwork under the guidance of teachers. This approach enables them to actively pursue scientific knowledge through inquiry-based learning methods, ultimately preparing them to comprehend the ever-evolving essence of the scientific method. However, it would be optimal for the researchers to understand the degree to which teacher interference can affect on the students' cognitive development, which needs to be addressed in the future.

2.3 The Relationship Between Scientific Inquiry and Problem-Solving Skills

Inquiry-based learning (IBL) courses effectively enhance students' critical thinking, interpersonal, and collaboration skills by utilizing intentionally designed problems or scenarios. Unlike rote learning, IBL fosters inquiry, investigative, and problem-solving abilities (Harada & Yoshina, 2004). Roesch et al. (2015) emphasize the need for further research to clarify the optimal methods, levels of guidance, and contexts for cultivating experimental problem-solving skills, especially for average or lower-performing groups. Take, for example, the study by (Klahr & Li, 2005) examined instructional methods for teaching variable control concepts to students in grades 3–5. Their study found that direct instruction, which included explicit, structured teaching, resulted in quicker and more effective learning outcomes compared to less guided approaches. This highlights the critical role of social interventions in deepening conceptual understanding, aligning with the principles of RCT.

In primary stages, problem solving is extensively practiced in mathematics domain. Within this curriculum, solving and posing problems stand out as crucial skills. Problem-solving involves identifying suitable solutions for novel and intricate situations, drawing upon students' existing knowledge. On the other hand, problem-posing entails generating fresh questions or challenges to explore specific scenarios and devising new problems rooted in the solutions to existing ones (Cai & Hwang, 2002; English, 2003). Engaging in problem-solving is a valuable learning journey that broadens, enhances, and reinforces one's understanding of mathematics. Equally crucial is the practice of problem-posing, which represents a significant undertaking in mathematical exploration extending beyond the realm of problem-solving proficiency (Gonzales, 1998; Silver & Cai, 2005). Researchers asserted that a strong correlation exists within solving problems and inquiry driven posing of problems for advancing in numerical reasoning and imagination, mutually reinforcing each other (Gonzales, 1998; Kilpatrick, 1987; Rosli et al., 2013).

In order to equip students with solving and posing problem abilities, the essential fact is to approach solving and posing problem in terms of a procedural aspect in contrast to simply the topics in the subject or assignment. Hence, it is crucial to structure learning environments in a manner that engages students in creative problem-solving. Recognizing the importance in fostering skills in solving and posing problems comprehensively, classrooms should be designed to enable students to tackle problems through diverse approaches. Moreover, students should be encouraged to effortlessly communicate their perspectives on processes including solving and posing problems between learners and mentors. To achieve this objective, various learning environments were experimented in diverse prior studies to assess students' abilities in problem solving and generating problems, wherein it was observed that the research-driven learning method motivates learners in generating individual questions as well as organizing their understanding (Ahmad et al., 2021; Ammar et al.,

2024). Prior studies also advocated on the positive effect of IBL on learners' behaviors, interest in activities and thereafter reducing their anxiety levels (Lazonder & Harmsen, 2016; Zweers et al., 2019).

Research also highlighted an importance in establishing conditions that empower students to consciously cultivate their metacognitive knowledge and skills, allowing them to effectively oversee and direct their individual understanding (Hartman, 2001). In the realm of mathematics education, another valuable component is metacognition, characterized by the act of reflecting on one's thought processes (Desoete & De Craene, 2019). Metacognition involves understanding the organization and functioning of an individual's mental abilities, along with ones strategizing, supervising and evaluating procedures while tackling the numerical reasoning. Employing metacognitive strategies fosters a conducive classroom atmosphere, fostering an enhancement in the mental abilities of students empowering accountability in acquiring knowledge. These strategies encompass a set of methods aimed at regulating cognitive efficiency in pursuit of a defined objective. Hence, students can engage in essential planning, monitoring, and evaluation of their learning processes throughout these procedures. Therefore, it is valuable to undertake thorough experiments in the applying approaches to improve the mental ability of students in the primary level of schooling. Research findings indicate that employing the IBL method with the support of metacognitive strategies proves efficient in enhancing the skills of students in solving and posing problems (Divrik et al., 2020).

Recently, Roesch et al. (2015) investigated how inquiry-based teaching could enhance the abilities of solving problems among German students from grade 6, yielding meaningful outcomes. Their study focused on engaging learners in solving problems in system ecology theoretical domain, employing a blend between direct instruction and open experimentation. They discovered that this approach supported specific facets in the ability to solve problems, such as creating cognitive inquiries, devising experiments of two-factors and recognizing appropriate control of experiments. The effects were somewhat minor, which was linked to their intricate nature within the intellectual field which was addressed. The findings were relevant for a broader understanding concerning the impact of conceptual fields, particularly in mentoring knowledge of scientific importance. Some research emphasizes developing abilities within a particular area of research to nurture scientific expertise and conceptual understanding. Conversely, other studies prioritize research methods and skills, relating concepts of scientific importance to a secondary position. The latter population highlights the importance of working across domains, tackling general problems across different scientific disciplines, to foster skill development and their transferability.

We conducted an inquiry driven problem-based teaching intervention including experiments that were built from a similar structure to solve problems within four procedures in four different workshops (Alkair et al., 2023). The study conducted on 202 primary students describes a problem-solving approach to engage learners in a sustainable event related to environment that integrates STEM subjects. The program includes four different workshops, each with experiments to solve problems through four procedures: (1) problem identification, (2) proposing suggestions, (3) testing and

(4) choosing the best solution. The program instructional design included educational tools that conferred an interactive learning environment through multimedia, practical experiments, procedures and educational games. The feedback mechanism by facilitators projected the program in a student-centered manner, thereby increasing their motivation to develop projects and design poster leading, meanwhile developing metacognitive skills including problem solving. We developed the theoretical framework on the principles of RCT wherein learning environment is pivotal in enhancing the student engagement as they work collaboratively under the guidance of facilitators (social interference) This study also embeds digital technology in an integrated curriculum from cross disciplines like science mathematics, engineering and technology. With the technology hype along the onset of pandemic in 2020, it became important in embracing technology's involvement in the development of these metacognitive skills under an inquiry driven approach.

2.4 Unraveling the Influence of Digital Technology on Research and Problem-Based Learning in Primary Skills

IBL revolves around questions, serving as the foundation of the entire learning journey and researchers have discovered that putting forward challenges, learners obtained effective strategic thinking abilities with an aptitude that determines the origin to examine individual conception. Learners, while generating questions, develop objectivity towards content, key areas of investigation and reflection through problem-based activities (Chin & Brown, 2002). Nevertheless, there are inherent difficulties in adopting inquiry-driven learning, including issues related to motivation, accessibility of investigative techniques, communication of results, alignment with curricular goals, and the incorporation of multiple representations. Researchers have delineated these five major obstacles and offered design tactics to tackle them by leveraging scientific visualization technology and curriculum planning (Edelson et al., 1999).

Recent technological advancements have generated a great deal of excitement among mentors and scholars, leading in the development of research-driven experiments in classrooms that underline the integration of technology in education. With a rapid advancement in digital tools and resources, educators are reimagining the way young learners engage with the curriculum. In this section of digital technology-based inquiry in primary education, we will delve into the technological influence on mentoring and grasping, and the innovative approaches being taken to integrate digital tools into the classroom to promote research and inquiry. By examining these aspects, hopefully a comprehensive knowledge about the evolving structure in inquiry driven primary education in the digital era will be obtained.

A study performed in Turkey investigated the reasons lying beneath the impact of Technology-Enhanced Problem-based Learning Activities (TEPLA) on attitudes of students and their achievements on mathematics offered insights on meaningful approaches to enhance contextual motivation and retention in the respective subject (Cetin et al., 2019). This study was grounded in the theoretical framework under RCT as TEPLA served as the maneuver to enhance their attitudes towards mathematics. In this case, the teacher employed TEPLA to instruct primary students in teaching mathematical functions by fostering an understanding of the practical applications and importance of functions in real-life mathematical scenarios. Here, the environment was built to simulate real life scenarios wherein the learners and instructors could easily build a rapport, which inherently caused to develop their motivation. The teacher played a facilitative role by illustrating real-life situations transformed into problem scenarios relevant to the subject matter. Learners engaged in small and large group discussions which indeed created a social ambiance between peers, aiming to draw mathematical conclusions from these examples.

A similar study was also conducted in Turkey that explored the impact of Technology-Based Inquiry Approach (TIBIA) in learning science subject for 5th grade primary students (Türkmen, 2009). Among the sample population of primary learners, the teacher employed a technology-driven inquiry method, prompting students to share their existing knowledge and express their curiosity. TBIA encompasses diverse activities, such as inspecting and deliberating on scientific concepts, employing novel representations like graphs, and performing collaborative work. Essential tools in TBIA involve inquiry investigations, hands-on tasks, reading, brainstorming, teacher demonstrations, laboratory exercises, and educational technologies like films and videos, all of which play pivotal roles when employed effectively. Diverse technology-driven activities and explorations included engaging learners in interactive simulations and animations for conducting scientific data collection and analyzing gathered data. TIBIA also fosters cooperative learning through online forums, virtual spaces, and social media and facilitate collaborative problem-solving via interactive whiteboards. Implementing WebQuest learning activities and utilizing web-based inquiry-science environments engaged students in conducting online investigations and undertaking internet-based research. Furthermore, the integration of these technologies aids learners in cultivating scientific literacy and honing critical thinking skills, which are crucial for addressing intricate challenges and making well-informed decisions. TBIA functions as a comprehensive concept intertwined with teaching and learning embracing techniques aimed at enhancing students' motivation. The teacher actively attended to students' queries and ideas, guiding them in discovering solutions to problems or addressing questions and the lesson plan was subsequently crafted based on the students' input, following a student-centered approach. Interactive media and computerized databases were employed in a 5E (engage, explore, explain, elaborate, evaluate) inquiry approach which facilitated the learners to enhance their inquiry skills as they proposed research ideas, developed supporting data leading to a train of thinking that further posed questions. This dynamic technology-based environment was crucial to developing their thinking skills and problem tackling approach based on motivation and interest.

However, there are challenges in incorporating ICT into classrooms in developing countries due to varying reasons such as lack of digital resources, internet, trained faculty etc. This was addressed by Stanford University as they developed in classrooms an arrangement to interconnect research-driven interventions and ICT module called the Stanford Mobile Inquiry-based Learning Environment (SMILE). The SMILE framework represented an educational advancement leveraging wireless advancements in fostering research-driven understanding within classroom environments, thereby promising accessibility to digitally underprivileged population. This innovative approach integrates a mobile application for learners in generating questions with multiple options in class hours and a corresponding management application for teachers. Through this system, students can share their questions with both peers and the mentors. This mobile application enables learners in exchanging, responding, and evaluating answers by scales like innovation and detailed examination. In summary, SMILE effectively stimulates student inquiry and transforms the dynamics between students and teachers in the classroom, which indeed aligns to the principles of RCT. A similar study performed on primary school students employed a learning application "AIBASE", for developing research questions while performing scientific trials (Ruzaman, 2020). This application by the researchers was aimed in the design of a pedagogy that scrutinizes the effective usage of "AIBASE" in supporting processes in education. The output showed an increase in the performance level of the students.

Apart from IBL integrated in science and mathematics, technology has made remarkable strides and ushered in substantial transformations in the field of social science especially in the instruction of languages like English. Incorporation of technology within EFL (English as a Foreign Language) education was widely acknowledged with an unquestionably enhanced mentoring and acquiring experiences (Mohammed, 2015). Indispensability of technology in English Language Learning has led to the emergence of more creative language teaching approaches. Also, technology offers an indefinite array of resources, enhancing the learning experience by providing motivation and stimulation for learners (Delgado et al., 2015). E-reading opens limitless opportunities, with a wealth of materials available online, granting students access to eBooks whenever necessary. Beyond just improving reading skills, e-reading cultivates a broader interest and motivation for reading among students. The noteworthy aspect is that digital learning provides numerous advantages for language learners. Introducing digital tools within EFL sessions not only boosts the interest and motivation of students but also aligns with their preference for working and reading through digital applications over traditional textbooks (Cutter, 2015). Hoven (1999) emphasizes that technology provides increasingly captivating resources, unquestionably offering learners significant opportunities to enhance their autonomy. Contemporary devices instill a sense of freedom and encouragement in students, thereby fostering increased motivation, activity, and engagement in the process of acquiring knowledge (Ilter, 2009). E-books facilitate the engagement of language learners in reading, fostering heightened motivation, interest, and a proclivity for extended reading activities. The utilization of e-books unquestionably amplifies enthusiasm for reading, leading to substantial enhancements in students' reading proficiency, comprehension, vocabulary acquisition, and overall attitude towards reading. These developments are integral for students to cultivate success and enthusiasm as readers (Khabeishvili, 2023). Examining digital applications appears to captivate the current generation, as they perceive eBooks to be contemporary, distinctive, and aesthetically appealing. This generation displays a keen enthusiasm for exploring diverse digital reading options, thereby cultivating an increasing interest in the overall reading experience. Furthermore, students' engagement can be heightened when presented with the opportunity to engage with eBooks that align with their proficiency levels and personal interests.

2.5 Chapter Summary

In this chapter, the focus is on the transformative role of curiosity and inquiry-driven learning in shaping the intellectual and cognitive development of primary learners. Curiosity, as a natural human trait, drives exploration and inquiry, serving as a critical component in fostering a mindset attuned to questioning and discovery. Inquiry-Based Learning (IBL) is introduced as a framework that channels this curiosity into meaningful educational experiences, enabling students to bridge theoretical knowledge with practical applications. By encouraging learners to identify knowledge gaps, engage in reflective inquiry, and collaboratively solve problems, IBL fosters critical thinking and intellectual engagement across disciplines, from science to language learning. Research highlights the effectiveness of curiosity-driven approaches, showcasing their potential to cultivate self-directed learning and a lifelong commitment to knowledge acquisition.

The chapter further delves into the significance of scientific inquiry as a hands-on, learner-centered approach, emphasizing the importance of creating environments that balance guidance with autonomy. Studies demonstrate that well-designed IBL interventions enhance students' experimental and problem-solving skills while fostering metacognitive awareness. Through practical activities, learners develop a deeper understanding of scientific concepts and processes, building a foundation for critical thinking and intellectual growth. Research-based education, when integrated into primary learning settings, not only strengthens cognitive abilities but also instills a sense of responsibility and independence in learners. By highlighting examples of successful IBL practices, the discussion underscores the critical role of inquiry in nurturing scientific thinking and developing skills vital for lifelong learning.

A gradual exploration of digital technology's integration into IBL illustrates its potential to enrich educational experiences further. Tools such as interactive simulations, mobile applications, and collaborative digital platforms offer innovative ways to engage learners and enhance their inquiry-driven education. Programs like SMILE and Technology-Enhanced Problem-Based Learning Activities (TEPLA) demonstrate how technology can overcome resource constraints, motivate learners, and foster collaborative exploration. While challenges remain in adopting such approaches universally, the potential for digital tools to transform traditional education, foster curiosity, and nurture self-regulated learners is significant. This chapter builds on these insights to advocate for a holistic, research-driven approach to primary education that bridges curiosity, scientific inquiry, and technological innovation.

Glossary

Term Definition

Curiosity A natural human trait driving exploration, questioning, and discovery, critical for intellectual growth

Inquiry-Based Learning (IBL) A hands-on, learner-centered approach focusing on exploration, questioning, and problem-solving

Research-Driven Learning An educational method emphasizing investigation and critical inquiry as part of the learning process

Information-Gap Decision Theory A theory suggesting that curiosity arises from a perceived lack of knowledge, motivating learners to seek answers

Scientific Inquiry A process where learners engage in experimentation, critical analysis, and evidence-based reasoning to explore phenomena

Problem-Solving The ability to identify, analyze, and resolve challenges using critical thinking and existing knowledge

Problem-Posing Generating new questions or challenges for exploration, often leading to deeper understanding and creativity

Epistemic Curiosity A strong desire to acquire new intellectual knowledge, motivating deep exploration and learning

Planned Behavior Theory A framework that identifies factors influencing a person's intentions and behaviors, such as cognitive understanding and self-efficacy

Metacognition Awareness and regulation of one's cognitive processes, aiding in planning, monitoring, and evaluating learning strategies

Technology-Enhanced Problem-Based Learning Activities (TEPLA) Educational interventions leveraging digital tools to enhance problem-solving and contextual learning

Technology-Based Inquiry Approach (TBIA) A technology-driven method promoting collaborative, hands-on learning and critical thinking in science education

Stanford Mobile Inquiry-Based Learning Environment (SMILE) A mobile learning framework enabling students to generate, share, and discuss questions in a classroom setting

5E Inquiry Model An instructional framework comprising Engage, Explore, Explain, Elaborate, and Evaluate phases to promote inquiry-based learning

Digital Learning Tools Resources such as simulations, e-books, and educational applications used to enhance student engagement and learning

EFL (English as a Foreign Language) The study of English by non-native speakers, often enhanced through digital tools and inquiry-driven approaches

Interactive Simulations Digital tools that replicate real-world scenarios for learners to explore and experiment with concepts

Collaborative Digital Platforms Online environments fostering group discussions, collaborative learning, and problem-solving activities

Self-Regulated Learning A process where learners set goals, monitor progress, and reflect on outcomes, promoting independence and responsibility

Dynamic Learning Environment An adaptable educational setting that integrates technology, inquiry, and collaboration to enhance learning outcomess

References

Abd-El-Khalick, F., BouJaoude, S., Duschl, R., Lederman, N. G., Mamlok-Naaman, R., Hofstein, A., Niaz, M., Treagust, D., & Tuan, H.-l. (2004). Inquiry in science education: International perspectives. *Science education, 88*(3), 397–419. https://doi.org/10.1002/sce.10118

Ahmad, Z., Ammar, M., & Al-Thani, N. J. (2021). Pedagogical models to implement effective stem research experience programs in high school students. *Education Sciences, 11*(11), 743.

Akuma, F. V., & Callaghan, R. (2019). A systematic review characterizing and clarifying intrinsic teaching challenges linked to inquiry-based practical work. *Journal of Research in Science Teaching, 56*(5), 619–648.

Alkair, S., Ali, R., Abouhashem, A., Aledamat, R., Bhadra, J., Ahmad, Z., Sellami, A., & Al-Thani, N. J. (2023, January 02). A STEM model for engaging students in environmental sustainability programs through a problem-solving approach. *Applied Environmental Education & Communication, 22*(1), 13–26. https://doi.org/10.1080/1533015X.2023.2179556

Ammar, M., Al-Thani, N. J., & Ahmad, Z. (2024). Role of pedagogical approaches in fostering innovation among K-12 students in STEM education. *Social Sciences & Humanities Open, 9*, 100839.

Areepattamannil, S. (2012, February 01). Effects of inquiry-based science instruction on science achievement and interest in science: Evidence from qatar. *The Journal of Educational Research, 105*(2), 134–146. https://doi.org/10.1080/00220671.2010.533717

Arnone, M. P., Grabowski, B. L., & Rynd, C. P. (1994). Curiosity as a personality variable influencing learning in a learner controlled lesson with and without advisement. *Educational Technology Research and Development, 42*(1), 5–20.

Buch, N., & Wolff, T. (2000). Classroom teaching through inquiry. *Journal of Professional Issues in Engineering Education and Practice, 126*(3), 105–109.

Bybee, R. W. (2014). NGSS and the next generation of science teachers. *Journal of Science Teacher Education, 25*(2), 211–221.

References

Cai, J., & Hwang, S. (2002). Generalized and generative thinking in US and Chinese students' mathematical problem solving and problem posing. *The Journal of Mathematical Behavior, 21*(4), 401–421.

Cetin, Y., Mirasyedioglu, S., & Cakiroglu, E. (2019). An inquiry into the underlying reasons for the impact of technology enhanced problem-based learning activities on students' attitudes and achievement. *Eurasian Journal of Educational Research, 19*(79), 191–208.

Chen, Z., & Klahr, D. (1999). All other things being equal: Acquisition and transfer of the control of variables strategy. *Child Development, 70*(5), 1098–1120.

Chin, C., & Brown, D. E. (2002). Student-generated questions: A meaningful aspect of learning in science. *International Journal of Science Education, 24*(5), 521–549.

Cremin, T., Glauert, E., Craft, A., Compton, A., & Stylianidou, F. (2018). Creative little scientists: Exploring pedagogical synergies between inquiry-based and creative approaches in early years science. In *Creativity and creative pedagogies in the early and primary years* (pp. 45–60). Routledge.

Cutter, M. (2015). Using technology with English language learners in the classroom.

Dean Jr, D., & Kuhn, D. (2007). Direct instruction vs. discovery: The long view. *Science education, 91*(3), 384–397.

Delgado, A. J., Wardlow, L., McKnight, K., & O'Malley, K. (2015). Educational technology: A review of the integration, resources, and effectiveness of technology in K-12 classrooms. *Journal of Information Technology Education: Research, 14*.

Desoete, A., & De Craene, B. (2019). Metacognition and mathematics education: An overview. *ZDM, 51*, 565–575.

Di Mauro, M. F., & Furman, M. (2016). Impact of an inquiry unit on grade 4 students' science learning. *International Journal of Science Education, 38*(14), 2239–2258.

Divrik, R., Pilten, P., & Tas, A. M. (2020). Effect of inquiry-based learning method supported by metacognitive strategies on fourth-grade students' problem-solving and problem-posing skills: A mixed methods research. *International Electronic Journal of Elementary Education, 13*(2), 287–308.

Dobber, M., Zwart, R., Tanis, M., & van Oers, B. (2017). Literature review: The role of the teacher in inquiry-based education. *Educational Research Review, 22*, 194–214.

Edelson, D. C., Gordin, D. N., & Pea, R. D. (1999). Addressing the challenges of inquiry-based learning through technology and curriculum design. *Journal of the learning sciences*, 391–450.

English, L. (2003). Mathematical modelling with young learners. In *Mathematical modelling* (pp. 3–17). Elsevier.

Ergül, R., Şımşeklı, Y., Çalış, S., Özdılek, Z., Göçmençelebı, Ş., & Şanli, M. (2011). The effects of inquiry-based science teaching on elementary school students' science process skills and science attitudes. *Bulgarian Journal of Science & Education Policy, 5*(1).

Furman, M. G. (2012). ¿ Qué ciencia estamos enseñando en escuelas de contextos de pobreza?

Furtak, E. M., Seidel, T., Iverson, H., & Briggs, D. C. (2012). Experimental and quasi-experimental studies of inquiry-based science teaching: A meta-analysis. *Review of Educational Research, 82*(3), 300–329.

Gillies, R. M., Nichols, K., Burgh, G., & Haynes, M. (2012). The effects of two strategic and meta-cognitive questioning approaches on children's explanatory behaviour, problem-solving, and learning during cooperative, inquiry-based science. *International Journal of Educational Research, 53*, 93–106.

Glogger-Frey, I., Fleischer, C., Grüny, L., Kappich, J., & Renkl, A. (2015). Inventing a solution and studying a worked solution prepare differently for learning from direct instruction. *Learning and Instruction, 39*, 72–87.

Gonzales, N. A. (1998). A blueprint for problem posing. *School Science and Mathematics, 98*(8), 448–456.

Harada, V. H., & Yoshina, J. M. (2004). Inquiry learning through librarian-teacher partnerships. *(No Title)*.

Harlen, W. (2000). Assessment in the inquiry classroom. *About Foundations, 2*, 87.

Hartman, H. J. (2001). Developing students' metacognitive knowledge and skills. *Metacognition in Learning and Instruction: Theory, Research and Practice*, 33–68.

Hoven, D. (1999). CALL-ing the learner into focus: Towards a learner-centred model for CALL. In. Swets & Zeitlinger.

Ilter, B. G. (2009). Effect of technology on motivation in EFL classrooms. *Turkish Online Journal of Distance Education, 10*(4), 136–158.

Jirout, J., & Klahr, D. (2012). Children's scientific curiosity: In search of an operational definition of an elusive concept. *Developmental Review, 32*(2), 125–160.

Kaberman, Z., & Dori, Y. J. (2009). Question posing, inquiry, and modeling skills of chemistry students in the case-based computerized laboratory environment. *International Journal of Science and Mathematics Education, 7*, 597–625.

Khabeishvili, G. (2023). Application of student-centered teaching methods in the classroom (a case of higher education institutions in Georgia). *Polylogue. Neophilological Studies, 13*(13), 183–198.

Kilpatrick, J. (1987). Problem formulating: Where do good problems come from? *Cognitive science and mathematics education*, 123–147.

Klahr, D., & Li, J. (2005). Cognitive research and elementary science instruction: From the laboratory, to the classroom, and back. *Journal of Science Education and Technology, 14*, 217–238.

Klahr, D., & Nigam, M. (2004). The equivalence of learning paths in early science instruction: Effects of direct instruction and discovery learning. *Psychological Science, 15*(10), 661–667.

Klahr, D., Zimmerman, C., & Jirout, J. (2011). Educational interventions to advance children's scientific thinking. *Science, 333*(6045), 971–975.

Lauriola, M., Litman, J. A., Mussel, P., De Santis, R., Crowson, H. M., & Hoffman, R. R. (2015). Epistemic curiosity and self-regulation. *Personality and Individual Differences, 83*, 202–207.

Lazonder, A. W., & Harmsen, R. (2016). Meta-analysis of inquiry-based learning: Effects of guidance. *Review of Educational Research, 86*(3), 681–718.

Lin, H. S., Hong, Z. R., & Cheng, Y. Y. (2009). The interplay of the classroom learning environment and inquiry-based activities. *International Journal of Science Education, 31*(8), 1013–1024.

McElhaney, K. W., & Linn, M. C. (2011). Investigations of a complex, realistic task: Intentional, unsystematic, and exhaustive experimenters. *Journal of Research in Science Teaching, 48*(7), 745–770.

Mohammed, M. İ. (2015). The perceptions of students and teachers about the benefits of and barriers to technology aided EFL. *Istanbul Aydin University Institute of Social Sciences*.

Muis, K. R., Pekrun, R., Sinatra, G. M., Azevedo, R., Trevors, G., Meier, E., & Heddy, B. C. (2015). The curious case of climate change: Testing a theoretical model of epistemic beliefs, epistemic emotions, and complex learning. *Learning and Instruction, 39*, 168–183.

Nichols, K., Burgh, G., & Kennedy, C. (2017). Comparing two inquiry professional development interventions in science on primary students' questioning and other inquiry behaviours. *Research in Science Education, 47*, 1–24.

Osborne, J., Simon, S., Collins, S., & Collins, S. (2003). Attitudes towards science: A review of the literature and its implications. *International Journal of Science Education, 25*(9), 1049–1079.

Oudeyer, P.-Y., Gottlieb, J., & Lopes, M. (2016). Intrinsic motivation, curiosity, and learning: Theory and applications in educational technologies. *Progress in Brain Research, 229*, 257–284.

Ozkal, K., Tekkaya, C., Cakiroglu, J., & Sungur, S. (2009). A conceptual model of relationships among constructivist learning environment perceptions, epistemological beliefs, and learning approaches. *Learning and Individual Differences, 19*(1), 71–79.

Post, T., & van der Molen, J. H. W. (2018). Do children express curiosity at school? Exploring children's experiences of curiosity inside and outside the school context. *Learning, Culture and Social Interaction, 18*, 60–71.

Post, T., & van der Molen, J. H. W. (2021). Effects of an inquiry-focused school improvement program on the development of pupils' attitudes towards curiosity, their implicit ability and effort beliefs, and goal orientations. *Motivation and Emotion, 45*, 13–38.

References

Roesch, F., Nerb, J., & Riess, W. (2015). Promoting experimental problem-solving ability in sixth-grade students through problem-oriented teaching of ecology: Findings of an intervention study in a complex domain. *International Journal of Science Education, 37*(4), 577–598.

Rönnebeck, S., Bernholt, S., & Ropohl, M. (2016). Searching for a common ground–A literature review of empirical research on scientific inquiry activities. *Studies in Science Education, 52*(2), 161–197.

Rosli, R., Goldsby, D., & Capraro, M. M. (2013). Assessing students' mathematical problem-solving and problem-posing skills. *Asian Social Science, 9*(16), 54.

Ruzaman, N. (2020). Inquiry-based education: Innovation in participatory inquiry paradigm. *International Journal of Emerging Technologies in Learning (iJET), 15*(10), 4–15.

Shymansky, J. A., Kyle Jr, W. C., & Alport, J. M. (2003). The effects of new science curricula on student performance. *Journal of Research in Science Teaching, 40*.

Silver, E. A., & Cai, J. (2005). Assessing students' mathematical problem posing. *Teaching Children Mathematics, 12*(3), 129–135.

Trevors, G. J., Muis, K. R., Pekrun, R., Sinatra, G. M., & Muijselaar, M. M. (2017). Exploring the relations between epistemic beliefs, emotions, and learning from texts. *Contemporary Educational Psychology, 48*, 116–132.

Türkmen, H. (2009). An effect of technology based inquiry approach on the learning of" Earth, Sun, & Moon" subject. *Asia-Pacific Forum on Science Learning & Teaching*.

Wilson, J., & Murdoch, K. (2016). *Helping your pupils to think for themselves*. Routledge.

Wu, J.-W., Tseng, J. C., & Hwang, G.-J. (2015). Development of an inquiry-based learning support system based on an intelligent knowledge exploration approach. *Journal of Educational Technology & Society, 18*(3), 282–300.

Zion, M. i., & Sadeh, I. (2007). Curiosity and open inquiry learning. *Journal of Biological Education, 41*(4), 162–169.

Zweers, I., Huizinga, M., Denessen, E., & Raijmakers, M. (2019). Inquiry-based learning for all: A systematic review of the effects of inquiry-based learning on knowledge, skills, attitudes and behavior of students with social-emotional and behavioral difficulties in primary and secondary education.

Open Access This chapter is licensed under the terms of the Creative Commons Attribution 4.0 International License (http://creativecommons.org/licenses/by/4.0/), which permits use, sharing, adaptation, distribution and reproduction in any medium or format, as long as you give appropriate credit to the original author(s) and the source, provide a link to the Creative Commons license and indicate if changes were made.

The images or other third party material in this chapter are included in the chapter's Creative Commons license, unless indicated otherwise in a credit line to the material. If material is not included in the chapter's Creative Commons license and your intended use is not permitted by statutory regulation or exceeds the permitted use, you will need to obtain permission directly from the copyright holder.

Chapter 3
Driving Project-Based Learning and Problem-Based Learning Through Research in Middle Schools

Abstract Chapter 3, titled "Driving Project-based Learning and Problem-based Learning through Research in Middle Schools," explores the integration of Research Cognitive Theory (RCT) within Project-based Learning (PBL) and Problem-based Learning (PBL) frameworks in middle school settings. This chapter provides an in-depth analysis of how RCT can enhance these pedagogical approaches to foster critical skills and attitudes among students. The chapter begins by discussing the theoretical foundations and practical applications of PBL and PBL, detailing how these methods support inquiry, collaboration, and real-world problem-solving. It presents case studies and practical examples to demonstrate how RCT can be effectively integrated into middle school curricula, thereby engaging students in meaningful, research-driven projects that promote critical thinking, creativity, and self-directed learning. Furthermore, the chapter highlights the crucial role of educational technology in advancing these pedagogical strategies. It reviews how technology can facilitate innovative, hands-on research experiences, support collaborative efforts, and provide students with tools to conduct and present research effectively. The chapter also addresses the challenges and opportunities associated with integrating technology into PBL and PBL frameworks, offering solutions to enhance implementation. Overall, Chapter 3 emphasizes the transformative potential of combining RCT with PBL and PBL in middle school education. It provides valuable insights into how these approaches can drive student learning, foster essential skills, and prepare students for future academic and professional challenges.

3.1 Project-Based Learning and Problem-Based Learning in Middle Schools

Like discussed in chapter 1 and 2, Project-Based Learning (PjBL) and Problem-Based Learning (PBL) are innovative educational approaches that emphasize student-centered learning and inquiry. Both methodologies encourage students to engage actively in their learning process, fostering essential skills such as critical thinking, collaboration, and creativity. PjBL involves students working on a project over an extended period, which culminates in a final product, presentation, or performance. The primary focus of PjBL is on the process of inquiry, where students explore a question or challenge, engage in research, and apply their knowledge to create a tangible outcome. This approach helps students see the relevance of their studies in real-world contexts, as they tackle complex, authentic problems that require higher-order thinking skills and collaborative efforts. On the other hand, PBL revolves around students learning through the experience of solving an open-ended problem. In this approach, students are presented with a problem that does not have a straightforward solution, prompting them to engage in research, gather information, and collaborate to devise potential solutions. PBL encourages self-directed learning, as students take responsibility for their learning process, exploring various resources and strategies to understand and solve the problem at hand. Both methodologies share common features, including the emphasis on inquiry, the relevance of real-world contexts, and the development of collaborative skills (Kolmos, 2009). However, while PBL is often project-focused with a defined outcome, PBL is more centered on the process of problem-solving and critical thinking.

Middle school is a critical stage in student development, where learners transition from concrete operational thinking to more abstract reasoning. During this period, students are developing their identities and learning how to work collaboratively with others. Implementing PJBL and PBL in middle school curricula can significantly impact student engagement, motivation, and academic success. Engagement and motivation are crucial components of effective learning, particularly in middle school education. PJBL and PBL inherently capture students' interest by connecting educational experiences to real-world challenges. When students engage in projects and problems that resonate with their lives and communities, they become more invested in their studies and motivated to learn (Boss & Larmer, 2018). This connection to real-life scenarios not only heightens engagement but also fosters a sense of ownership over their learning process. As a result, students are likely to demonstrate improved academic outcomes, fueled by their intrinsic motivation to explore and succeed. In addition to boosting engagement, PjBL and PBL play a significant role in developing critical thinking and problem-solving skills (Anazifa & Djukri, 2017). In today's rapidly changing world, the ability to think critically and solve complex problems is essential for success. These methodologies encourage students to analyze the information they encounter, consider various perspectives, and synthesize knowledge to devise innovative solutions. Such skills are not merely academic; they are vital for students' future careers and civic responsibilities. By cultivating a mindset geared toward inquiry and analysis, students are better prepared to tackle the multifaceted challenges they will face in their personal and professional lives.

The emphasis on teamwork and effective communication in PjBL and PBL further enriches the educational experience. Both methodologies require students to work collaboratively in groups, where they share ideas, negotiate roles, and provide constructive feedback to one another. This collaborative environment not only fosters social skills but also teaches students how to articulate their thoughts clearly and listen to diverse viewpoints (Saleh et al., 2022; Zhang et al., 2009). These competencies are invaluable in any professional setting, where collaboration and communication are often key to achieving successful outcomes. By engaging in these collaborative learning experiences, students build essential interpersonal skills that will serve them well throughout their lives. Moreover, PjBL and PBL encourage self-directed learning, promoting a culture of inquiry that empowers students to ask questions, seek answers, and explore topics that pique their interest. This approach fosters a growth mindset, where students learn to embrace challenges and view failures not as setbacks but as opportunities for growth and development. By taking charge of their learning journey, students become active participants in the educational process, which enhances their confidence and perseverance (Safitri et al., 2024). The ability to pursue one's interests and navigate challenges independently prepares students for lifelong learning and adaptability in an ever-evolving world. In summary, the integration of PjBL and PBL in middle school education significantly enhances engagement and motivation, develops critical thinking and problem-solving skills, fosters collaboration and communication, and encourages self-directed learning. These methodologies create a rich, dynamic learning environment where students can thrive academically and personally, equipping them with the essential skills needed for future success.

Extensive research supports the effectiveness of PjBL and PBL in improving student outcomes. Studies have shown that these methodologies lead to enhanced academic performance, increased retention of knowledge, and greater motivation to learn. For instance, research indicates that students engaged in project-based learning demonstrate higher levels of understanding and application of content compared to those in traditional learning environments (Chen & Yang, 2019). Moreover, PjBL and PBL have been shown to improve essential skills such as collaboration, communication, and problem-solving (Hmelo-Silver, 2004; Kokotsaki et al., 2016). A meta-analysis of PjBL studies highlighted that students participating in PjBL experiences exhibited better teamwork and communication skills than their peers in traditional classrooms (Zhang & Ma, 2023). These findings underscore the importance of incorporating these pedagogical approaches into middle school curricula to prepare students for the complexities of modern society.

To effectively implement PjBL and PBL in middle schools, educators should consider several key strategies that foster an engaging and productive learning environment. First and foremost, curriculum alignment is essential. Educators must ensure that the projects and problems students encounter align with curricular standards and learning objectives. This alignment guarantees that students acquire the necessary knowledge and skills while engaging in meaningful learning experiences that are relevant to their academic growth. While PjBL and PBL inherently promote student autonomy, it is vital for educators to provide structured guidance and support throughout the learning process. Teachers play a crucial role in facilitating students' exploration by offering scaffolding, resources, and the necessary support to help them navigate challenges (Kudryashova et al., 2015). This may involve modeling research skills, facilitating discussions that encourage critical thinking, and offering constructive feedback during various stages of the project or problem-solving process. By guiding students effectively, educators can enhance their confidence and foster a deeper understanding of the subject matter.

Further, creating a collaborative learning environment is also fundamental to the success of PjBL and PBL. Establishing a culture of collaboration helps students develop essential social skills and teamwork abilities. Teachers can foster this collaborative spirit by encouraging group work, promoting respectful communication among peers, and establishing clear roles and responsibilities within each group. This structured collaboration not only enhances students' interpersonal skills but also ensures that they learn to articulate their ideas clearly and listen to others' perspectives, which are invaluable skills in both academic and professional settings. Moreover, the utilization of technology plays a significant role in enhancing the PjBL and PBL experience (Al-Abdullatif & Gameil, 2021). Integrating digital tools can facilitate various aspects of learning, including research, collaboration, and presentation. By leveraging technology, educators can enable students to connect with broader communities and access a wealth of resources that enrich their projects. The incorporation of technology not only enhances the overall learning experience but also prepares students for a future where digital literacy is essential.

Finally, effective assessment of process and product is crucial for PjBL and PBL. Educators should assess both the collaborative process and the final outcomes of students' work, providing feedback that encourages reflection and personal growth. Employing rubrics can be particularly helpful in evaluating students' collaborative efforts, critical thinking skills, and presentation abilities. This assessment strategy ensures that evaluations align with the learning objectives and provides students with clear expectations for their work. In summary, the successful implementation of PjBL and PBL in middle schools hinges on careful curriculum alignment, structured guidance, the creation of a collaborative environment, the integration of technology, and effective assessment strategies. By focusing on these key areas, educators can foster a dynamic and engaging learning atmosphere that promotes essential skills and prepares students for future challenges.

In conclusion, PjBL and PBL are powerful pedagogical approaches that can significantly enhance middle school education. By fostering engagement, critical thinking, collaboration, and self-directed learning, PjBL and PBL prepare students for the challenges of the 21st century. Educators are encouraged to embrace these methodologies, creating dynamic learning environments that inspire curiosity and a love for learning. As research continues to support the effectiveness of these approaches, the integration of PjBL and PBL into middle school curricula remains a vital strategy for nurturing the next generation of innovative thinkers and problem solvers.

3.2 The Integration of Research Cognitive Theory (RCT) into PjBL and PBL

Research Cognitive Theory (RCT) emphasizes the critical relationship between cognitive processes and research practices, illustrating how structured inquiry can enhance educational experiences. At its core, RCT posits that effective research experiences can foster the development of essential cognitive and social skills, preparing students for the complexities of the modern world. In the context of middle school education, RCT serves as a guiding framework for integrating research into pedagogical approaches like PBL and PjBL, enabling educators to cultivate a learning environment rich in inquiry and exploration. The application of RCT within these methodologies is particularly beneficial during middle school, a pivotal time when students transition from concrete operational thinking to more abstract reasoning. As students engage with research-driven learning experiences, they are not only encouraged to think critically but also to take ownership of their learning journey, leading to deeper cognitive engagement. Integrating RCT into PBL and PBL has been shown to significantly enhance student engagement. Research indicates that when students participate in inquiry-based projects that resonate with their interests and real-world challenges, their intrinsic motivation increases. For example, studies have found that middle school students engaged in research-oriented projects reported higher levels of interest and engagement, leading to improved academic performance and a deeper commitment to their studies bedding research into these methodologies (LaForce et al., 2017; Mohr-Schroeder et al., 2014; Wyss et al., 2012). One successful implementation involved a middle school project where students explored local environmental issues (Alkair et al., 2023). By framing the project around their community, students connected their research to real-world challenges, significantly boosting their motivation to learn and explore complex topics. This alignment of personal relevance with academic inquiry exemplifies how RCT can transform learning experiences.

A core aspect of RCT is its emphasis on fostering critical thinking and problem-solving abilities. Engaging students in PBL and PBL encourages them to analyze information, evaluate different perspectives, and devise innovative solutions to complex problems. Research shows that students exposed to research-driven educational settings demonstrate enhanced critical thinking skills compared to their peers in traditional classrooms (Gibson & Chase, 2002; Kang & Keinonen, 2018; Zimmerman, 2007). Another study conducted in a middle school, students engaged in a PBL unit focused on renewable energy sources (Anwar et al., 2024). They were tasked with developing a sustainable energy plan for their school, which required them to research various energy options, analyze data, and present their findings. This project not only developed their analytical skills but also encouraged them to apply theoretical knowledge to practical situations. As students collaborated to solve real-life challenges, they cultivated essential problem-solving skills that extend beyond the classroom. RCT also emphasizes the importance of collaboration and communication within the learning process. In both PBL and PBL frameworks, students frequently work in groups, where they share ideas, negotiate roles, and provide feedback to one another. This collaborative approach enhances their understanding of the content while helping them develop vital social skills. Studies have shown that students who engage in collaborative learning environments are better prepared for future teamwork situations (Hmelo-Silver et al., 2008; Ku et al., 2013). Therefore, collaborative experiences are essential, as they equip students with the interpersonal skills necessary for success in both academic and professional environments.

3.3 Educational Technology's Role in PjBL and PBL

Educational technology has become an integral component of modern teaching and learning strategies, particularly in middle school settings. The rise of digital tools and online resources has transformed the educational landscape, providing opportunities for enhanced engagement and deeper learning (Bagheri et al., 2013). In the context of PjBL and PBL, educational technology facilitates collaboration, research, and presentation, allowing students to access diverse resources and share their findings in innovative ways. By integrating technology into these pedagogical approaches, educators can create dynamic learning environments that foster inquiry and creativity. One of the primary benefits of incorporating technology into PjBL and PBL is its ability to enhance collaboration and communication among students (Spector, 2001). Digital platforms such as Google Workspace, Microsoft Teams, and various project management tools enable students to work together seamlessly, regardless of their physical location. These tools allow for real-time collaboration, where students can share documents, brainstorm ideas, and provide feedback instantly. Research supports the notion that technology-enhanced collaboration leads to improved learning outcomes (Chen & Chen, 2024). For instance, a study indicated that students who utilized collaborative tools during projects demonstrated higher levels of engagement and satisfaction compared to those who worked in traditional settings technology to facilitate teamwork, educators can help students develop essential communication skills and learn how to articulate their thoughts effectively within a group context (Ellaway, 2018; Gulati, 2008). Moreover, video conferencing platforms such as Zoom or Skype allow students to connect with experts or peers from different geographical locations. This exposure to diverse perspectives enriches the learning experience and broadens students' understanding of global issues. For example, in a project focused on climate change, students might collaborate with peers from other countries, sharing insights and solutions relevant to their local contexts.

Educational technology also plays a crucial role in supporting research and inquiry in PjBL and PBL. Access to online databases, e-books, and academic journals provides students with a wealth of information at their fingertips. Digital literacy skills are increasingly vital in today's information-rich environment, and integrating technology into research projects helps students learn how to evaluate sources critically and discern credible information. In a middle school project that investigates

3.3 Educational Technology's Role in PjBL and PBL

local history, for instance, students can utilize online archives, digital libraries, and multimedia resources to gather data and develop a deeper understanding of their research topics. This approach not only enhances their research skills but also encourages them to explore diverse perspectives and interpret information critically. Additionally, technology can facilitate data collection and analysis. Students can use tools like Google Forms for surveys or data collection, and software such as Excel or Google Sheets for organizing and analyzing their findings. These technological applications empower students to engage in authentic research practices, simulating real-world scientific inquiry processes. Studies have shown that when students are involved in hands-on research activities supported by technology, their interest in the subject matter significantly increases, leading to greater retention of knowledge (Ma & Nickerson, 2006; Wang et al., 2014).

In PjBL and PBL, presenting findings is a crucial step in the learning process. Educational technology provides students with various tools to create engaging presentations that effectively communicate their research outcomes. Platforms such as Prezi, Canva, and Google Slides allow students to design visually appealing presentations, incorporating multimedia elements like images, videos, and interactive content (Chou et al., 2015; Mayhew, 2019; Zahri & Rahmawati, 2024). The use of technology in presentations not only enhances the visual appeal but also engages diverse learning styles. For instance, students who may struggle with traditional presentation formats might find success through creative digital storytelling or video production. This flexibility encourages all students to express their understanding in ways that resonate with them, fostering a sense of ownership over their learning. Furthermore, technology facilitates broader sharing of students' work beyond the classroom. Online platforms and social media allow students to showcase their projects to a wider audience, including peers, parents, and the community (Sohoni, 2019; Willis & Exley, 2018). For example, a project on environmental conservation might culminate in a digital campaign where students share their findings and proposed solutions through blogs, videos, or social media posts. This not only reinforces the importance of their research but also empowers students to contribute to meaningful conversations within their communities.

Therefore, in summary, educational technology plays a pivotal role in enhancing PjBL and PBL by fostering collaboration, supporting research, and facilitating engaging presentations. By integrating technology thoughtfully, educators can create rich, dynamic learning environments that promote inquiry, creativity, and critical thinking among middle school students. As technology continues to evolve, its potential to transform educational practices and enrich student experiences remains significant. By addressing challenges associated with technology integration and providing students with the necessary resources and support, educators can empower the next generation of learners to thrive in an increasingly digital world.

3.4 Challenges and Opportunities in Implementation and Assessment Strategies

Implementing PjBL and PBL in middle schools presents a unique set of challenges that educators must navigate to create effective learning experiences. These challenges can stem from various sources, including institutional constraints, resource limitations, and varying levels of teacher preparedness (Devkota et al., 2017; Ferwati et al., 2023; Kokotsaki et al., 2016). Identifying and addressing these challenges is essential for successfully integrating these methodologies into the curriculum. One of the primary challenges is the alignment of curricular standards with project-based and problem-based approaches. Educators often struggle to align the objectives of these methodologies with mandated learning outcomes and standardized assessments. This misalignment can lead to difficulties in justifying the time spent on projects, particularly when administrators emphasize traditional testing methods over innovative teaching strategies. Moreover, the diverse needs of students in a middle school setting can pose significant hurdles. With varying learning styles, interests, and abilities, educators may find it challenging to design projects that cater to all students effectively. Ensuring that each student is engaged and challenged while also receiving the necessary support requires careful planning and differentiation, which can be time-consuming and complex.

Also, resource limitations can significantly impact the successful implementation of PjBL and PBL (Kokotsaki et al., 2016). Middle schools may face constraints related to funding, technology access, and materials needed for projects. Without adequate resources, teachers may be forced to modify or abandon their planned projects, leading to missed opportunities for meaningful learning experiences. In many cases, schools may lack the technology or equipment necessary for students to conduct research or collaborate effectively. For instance, if students do not have access to computers or reliable internet connections, they may struggle to gather information or communicate with peers and mentors. This lack of access can hinder students' ability to engage fully in the project-based learning process. Furthermore, teachers often require professional development to implement PjBL and PBL successfully. Without ongoing training and support, educators may feel unprepared to adopt these methodologies, leading to inconsistent implementation across classrooms. Professional development opportunities focused on best practices for project-based and problem-based learning can empower educators to design and facilitate engaging learning experiences that align with curricular standards.

Despite the challenges, the integration of PjBL and PBL presents numerous opportunities for innovative teaching practices. These methodologies encourage educators to embrace creativity and flexibility in their lesson planning, fostering an environment where students can explore topics that interest them and make meaningful connections to their learning. One significant opportunity lies in the potential for collaborative partnerships with local organizations and businesses (Boztepe, 2022; Stefl-Mabry et al., 2005). By engaging with community members, educators can

3.4 Challenges and Opportunities in Implementation and Assessment ...

provide students with authentic learning experiences that extend beyond the classroom (Willems & Gonzalez-DeHass, 2012). For example, partnering with local environmental organizations can enable students to work on projects related to sustainability and conservation, allowing them to apply their knowledge to real-world issues. Additionally, the emphasis on inquiry and exploration in PjBL and PBL allows educators to create interdisciplinary projects that integrate multiple subject areas (Brassler & Dettmers, 2017). This approach not only enhances students' understanding of the connections between different disciplines but also fosters critical thinking and problem-solving skills. For instance, a project on renewable energy could encompass science, math, and social studies, enabling students to analyze data, conduct experiments, and explore the societal implications of energy use.

For this, assessment is a crucial component of implementing PjBL and PBL effectively. Educators must develop strategies that evaluate both the process and the final product of students' work. Traditional assessment methods may not accurately reflect students' understanding and growth in a project-based learning environment. Therefore, educators need to employ innovative assessment strategies that align with the objectives of PjBL and PBL. Formative assessment plays a vital role in this context. By regularly assessing students throughout the project, educators can provide ongoing feedback that encourages reflection and improvement. This can involve peer assessments, self-reflections, and teacher observations, which allow students to articulate their learning experiences and identify areas for growth. Research has shown that when students receive timely feedback, they are more likely to improve their performance and deepen their understanding of the content (Van der Kleij et al., 2019). Additionally, rubrics can be beneficial in evaluating collaborative efforts, critical thinking, and presentation skills. Clear criteria outlined in rubrics help students understand expectations and provide a framework for assessment. This transparency allows students to take ownership of their learning and understand how to succeed in future projects. Engaging stakeholders, including parents and community members, in the assessment process can enhance the effectiveness of PjBL and PBL. By sharing students' projects with parents and inviting community members to participate in presentations or evaluations, educators can create a sense of accountability and pride in students' work. This involvement fosters a supportive learning environment where students feel valued and recognized for their efforts. Moreover, incorporating stakeholder feedback into the assessment process can provide valuable insights. Community members may offer different perspectives or expertise that enrich the learning experience. For instance, if students are working on a project related to local history, inviting a local historian to evaluate their findings can provide an authentic assessment experience and deepen students' understanding of the subject matter.

In conclusion, while implementing PjBL and PBL in middle schools presents various challenges, it also offers numerous opportunities for enhancing student engagement and learning outcomes. By understanding and addressing these challenges, educators can create effective implementation strategies that harness the benefits of project-based learning. Thoughtful assessment practices that focus on formative evaluation, clear criteria, and peer involvement can ensure that students are not only held accountable for their learning but are also encouraged to grow and develop their skills throughout the process. Ultimately, by overcoming obstacles and embracing the opportunities presented by PjBL and PBL, educators can foster a rich, inquiry-based learning environment that prepares students for the complexities of the 21st century.

3.5 Chapter Summary

In summary, in this chapter, the focus shifts to the dynamic role of Project-Based Learning (PjBL) and Problem-Based Learning (PBL) in middle school education, exploring their synergy with Research Cognitive Theory (RCT) to create an environment rich in inquiry and critical thinking. PjBL and PBL are introduced as transformative methodologies that emphasize student-centered learning by encouraging collaboration, critical analysis, and creativity. Middle school, being a critical stage of cognitive and social development, serves as an ideal platform for these approaches. PjBL engages students through extended projects culminating in tangible outcomes, while PBL focuses on solving open-ended problems, fostering self-directed learning. Both methods tap into real-world contexts to enhance student motivation, critical thinking, and problem-solving skills, as well as collaborative and communicative abilities. This active engagement not only prepares students for academic success but also instills a growth mindset, encouraging perseverance and adaptability in an ever-changing world.

The chapter delves into how RCT enhances these methodologies, emphasizing structured inquiry as a means to develop cognitive and social skills. By integrating RCT, educators create opportunities for students to explore topics that resonate with their interests, leading to deeper engagement and academic performance. Examples like environmental and renewable energy projects demonstrate how RCT aligns academic inquiry with real-world challenges, fostering critical thinking and collaborative problem-solving. The integration of educational technology is highlighted as a pivotal element in modernizing PjBL and PBL. Digital tools support collaboration, research, and presentations, enabling students to connect with broader communities and access diverse resources. These technologies empower students to critically evaluate information, develop research skills, and present findings creatively, fostering an interactive and enriching learning experience.

Finally, the chapter addresses the challenges and opportunities in implementing PjBL and PBL in middle school settings. Institutional constraints, resource limitations, and teacher preparedness are acknowledged as significant barriers, but they are counterbalanced by opportunities for interdisciplinary projects and collaborative partnerships with local organizations. Assessment is presented as a crucial component, with an emphasis on formative evaluation, rubrics, and stakeholder involvement to measure both the process and outcomes effectively. By addressing these challenges and embracing opportunities, educators can create robust inquiry-driven environments that prepare students for the complexities of the twenty-first century, equipping them with the essential skills and mindset for lifelong success.

Glossary

Term Definition

Project-Based Learning (PjBL) A student-centered approach where learners work on a project over an extended period, culminating in a final product or presentation

Problem-Based Learning (PBL) A methodology where students learn by solving open-ended problems, fostering critical thinking and self-directed learning

Research Cognitive Theory (RCT) A theoretical framework emphasizing the relationship between research practices and cognitive processes to enhance learning

Critical Thinking The ability to analyze, evaluate, and synthesize information to solve complex problems effectively

Collaboration Working with others to achieve shared goals, emphasizing teamwork, communication, and mutual respect

Self-Directed Learning An approach where learners take responsibility for their education, exploring topics and resources independently

Curriculum Alignment The process of ensuring that learning objectives, projects, and activities align with educational standards and goals

Educational Technology Digital tools and resources used to enhance teaching and learning experiences, including research, collaboration, and presentations

Formative Assessment An evaluation method that provides ongoing feedback to help students improve during the learning process

Rubrics Tools outlining criteria for assessment, helping students understand expectations and enabling consistent evaluation

Digital Literacy The ability to find, evaluate, and use digital tools and resources effectively for research and communication

Interdisciplinary Projects Learning activities that integrate concepts and skills from multiple subject areas to address complex, real-world challenges

Stakeholder Involvement The engagement of parents, community members, or industry experts in the learning process to provide feedback and support

Growth Mindset The belief in the ability to improve through effort, perseverance, and adaptability, particularly when facing challenges

Inquiry-Driven Learning An approach emphasizing exploration, questioning, and investigation to foster deep understanding and critical thinking

21st-Century Skills Competencies such as critical thinking, collaboration, communication, creativity, and problem-solving required for modern success

Google Workspace A suite of cloud-based collaboration tools, including Google Docs, Sheets, and Slides, often used in educational settings

SMILE Framework The Stanford Mobile Inquiry-based Learning Environment, a digital tool designed to promote inquiry and collaboration in classrooms

5E Inquiry Model An instructional framework with five phases: Engage, Explore, Explain, Elaborate, and Evaluate, promoting active learning

Social Interference The influence of collaboration and interaction with peers or mentors on a student's learning and development

Dynamic Learning Environment An adaptable and interactive educational setting that integrates technology, collaboration, and inquiry for enriched learning experiences

References

Al-Abdullatif, A. M., & Gameil, A. A. (2021). The effect of digital technology integration on students' academic performance through project-based learning in an e-learning environment. *International Journal of Emerging Technologies in Learning, 16*(11).

Alkair, S., Ali, R., Abouhashem, A., Aledamat, R., Bhadra, J., Ahmad, Z., Sellami, A., & Al-Thani, N. J. (2023). A STEM model for engaging students in environmental sustainability programs through a problem-solving approach. *Applied Environmental Education & Communication*, 1–14.

Anazifa, R. D., & Djukri, D. (2017). Project-based learning and problem-based learning: Are they effective to improve student's thinking skills? *Jurnal Pendidikan IPA Indonesia, 6*(2), 346–355.

Anwar, R., Elbashir, A. M., Magdy, R., Ahmad, Z., & Al-Thani, N. J. (2024). Effectiveness of STEM based workshop for deaf education: Exploratory study. *Heliyon, 10*(16).

Bagheri, M., Ali, W. Z. W., Abdullah, M. C. B., & Daud, S. M. (2013). Effects of project-based learning strategy on self-directed learning skills of educational technology students. *Contemporary educational technology, 4*(1), 15–29.

Boss, S., & Larmer, J. (2018). *Project based teaching: How to create rigorous and engaging learning experiences.* ASCD.

Boztepe, S. (2022). Organizational learning through collaborative project-based service design course: The flip side of the coin.

Brassler, M., & Dettmers, J. (2017). How to enhance interdisciplinary competence—interdisciplinary problem-based learning versus interdisciplinary project-based learning. *Interdisciplinary Journal of problem-based Learning, 11*(2).

Chen, C.-H., & Yang, Y.-C. (2019). Revisiting the effects of project-based learning on students' academic achievement: A meta-analysis investigating moderators. *Educational Research Review, 26*, 71–81.

Chen, F., & Chen, G. (2024). Technology-enhanced collaborative inquiry in K–12 classrooms: A systematic review of empirical studies. *Science & Education*, 1–43.

Chou, P.-N., Chang, C.-C., & Lu, P.-F. (2015). Prezi versus PowerPoint: The effects of varied digital presentation tools on students' learning performance. *Computers & education, 91*, 73–82.

Devkota, S. P., Giri, D. R., & Bagale, S. (2017). Developing 21st century skills through project-based learning in EFL context: challenges and opportunities. *The Online Journal of New Horizons in Education, 7*(1).

Ellaway, R. H. (2018). Technology-enhanced learning. *Understanding medical education: evidence, theory, and practice*, 139–149.

Ferwati, W., Junaidi, A., Napitupulu, E., & Hamid, A. (2023). Systematic review of literature: Advantages and challenges in implementing the Project-Based Learning (PjBL). *Cendikia: Media Jurnal Ilmiah Pendidikan, 14*(2), 160–166.

Gibson, H. L., & Chase, C. (2002). Longitudinal impact of an inquiry-based science program on middle school students' attitudes toward science. *Science education, 86*(5), 693–705. https://doi.org/10.1002/sce.10039

Gulati, S. (2008). Technology-enhanced learning in developing nations: A review. *The International Review of Research in Open and Distributed Learning, 9*(1).

Hmelo-Silver, C. E. (2004). Problem-based learning: What and how do students learn? *Educational psychology review, 16*, 235–266.

References

Hmelo-Silver, C. E., Chernobilsky, E., & Jordan, R. (2008). Understanding collaborative learning processes in new learning environments. *Instructional Science, 36*, 409–430.

Kang, J., & Keinonen, T. (2018). The effect of student-centered approaches on students' interest and achievement in science: Relevant topic-based, open and guided inquiry-based, and discussion-based approaches. *Research in Science Education, 48*, 865–885.

Kokotsaki, D., Menzies, V., & Wiggins, A. (2016). Project-based learning: A review of the literature. *Improving schools, 19*(3), 267–277.

Kolmos, A. (2009). Problem-based and project-based learning. *University science and mathematics education in transition*, 261–280.

Ku, H.-Y., Tseng, H. W., & Akarasriworn, C. (2013). Collaboration factors, teamwork satisfaction, and student attitudes toward online collaborative learning. *Computers in Human Behavior, 29*(3), 922–929.

Kudryashova, A., Gorbatova, T., Rybushkina, S., & Ivanova, E. (2015). Teacher's roles to facilitate active learning. *Mediterranean Journal of Social Sciences, 7*(1), 460–466.

LaForce, M., Noble, E., & Blackwell, C. (2017). Problem-based learning (PBL) and student interest in STEM careers: The roles of motivation and ability beliefs. *Education Sciences, 7*(4), 92.

Ma, J., & Nickerson, J. V. (2006). Hands-on, simulated, and remote laboratories: A comparative literature review. *ACM computing surveys (CSUR), 38*(3), 7-es.

Mayhew, E. (2019). The new generation of Prezi presentation software, provided by Prezi Inc., and student engagement and learning within political science. *Journal of Political Science Education, 15*(3), 406–409.

Mohr-Schroeder, M. J., Jackson, C., Miller, M., Walcott, B., Little, D. L., Speler, L., Schooler, W., & Schroeder, D. C. (2014). Developing middle school students' interests in STEM via summer learning experiences: S ee B lue STEM C amp. *School Science and Mathematics, 114*(6), 291–301.

Safitri, R., Wahyuri, A. S., & Ockta, Y. (2024). The impacts of the project-based learning and problem-based learning models with self-confidence on students' learning outcomes. *Indonesian Research Journal in Education| IRJE, 8*(1), 269–283.

Saleh, A., Phillips, T. M., Hmelo-Silver, C. E., Glazewski, K. D., Mott, B. W., & Lester, J. C. (2022). A learning analytics approach towards understanding collaborative inquiry in a problem-based learning environment. *British Journal of Educational Technology, 53*(5), 1321–1342.

Sohoni, T. (2019). Harnessing the power of social media in the classroom: Challenging students to create content to share on social media sites to improve learning outcomes. *Journal of Criminal Justice Education, 30*(3), 389–406.

Spector, J. M. (2001). An overview of progress and problems in educational technology. *Interactive educational multimedia: IEM*, 27–37.

Stefl-Mabry, J., Powers, J. G., & Doll, C. (2005). Creating and sustaining problem-based partnerships among graduate, undergraduate, and K-12 learners: Opportunities and challenges. *Journal of Educational Technology Systems, 34*(2), 131–153.

Van der Kleij, F. M., Adie, L. E., & Cumming, J. J. (2019). A meta-review of the student role in feedback. *International Journal of Educational Research, 98*, 303–323.

Wang, C.-Y., Wu, H.-K., Lee, S.W.-Y., Hwang, F.-K., Chang, H.-Y., Wu, Y.-T., Chiou, G.-L., Chen, S., Liang, J.-C., & Lin, J.-W. (2014). A review of research on technology-assisted school science laboratories. *Journal of Educational Technology & Society, 17*(2), 307–320.

Willems, P. P., & Gonzalez-DeHass, A. R. (2012). School-community partnerships: Using authentic contexts to academically motivate students. *School Community Journal, 22*(2), 9–30.

Willis, L., & Exley, B. (2018). Using an online social media space to engage parents in student learning in the early-years: Enablers and impediments. *Digital Education Review, 33*, 87–104.

Wyss, V. L., Heulskamp, D., & Siebert, C. J. (2012). Increasing middle school student interest in STEM careers with videos of scientists. *International Journal of Environmental and Science Education, 7*(4), 501–522.

Zahri, N. S., & Rahmawati, F. P. (2024). Strengthening presentation skills through TPACK-based canva media for elementary school students. *Jurnal Fundadikdas (Fundamental Pendidikan Dasar), 7*(1), 1–10.

Zhang, K., Peng, S. W., Hung, J., & l. (2009). Online collaborative learning in a project-based learning environment in Taiwan: A case study on undergraduate students' perspectives. *Educational Media International, 46*(2), 123–135.

Zhang, L., & Ma, Y. (2023). A study of the impact of project-based learning on student learning effects: A meta-analysis study. *Frontiers in psychology, 14*, 1202728.

Zimmerman, C. (2007). The development of scientific thinking skills in elementary and middle school. *Developmental Review, 27*(2), 172–223.

Open Access This chapter is licensed under the terms of the Creative Commons Attribution 4.0 International License (http://creativecommons.org/licenses/by/4.0/), which permits use, sharing, adaptation, distribution and reproduction in any medium or format, as long as you give appropriate credit to the original author(s) and the source, provide a link to the Creative Commons license and indicate if changes were made.

The images or other third party material in this chapter are included in the chapter's Creative Commons license, unless indicated otherwise in a credit line to the material. If material is not included in the chapter's Creative Commons license and your intended use is not permitted by statutory regulation or exceeds the permitted use, you will need to obtain permission directly from the copyright holder.

Chapter 4
Revolutionizing RCT in Highschool Through Research Experiences

Abstract This chapter, titled "Revolutionizing RCT in High School," examines the transformative potential of real-world experiential research in advancing Research Cognitive Theory (RCT) for pre-university students. It begins by reviewing historical research apprenticeship models and their impact on fostering independent learning and critical thinking among high school students. Despite their proven benefits, the chapter notes a significant gap in documentation regarding the cognitive behaviors cultivated through these models. The chapter introduces Research-Based Learning (RBL) as a pedagogical approach that incorporates authentic research activities into the high school curriculum. It provides empirical evidence demonstrating RBL's effectiveness in enhancing students' research capabilities, scientific inquiry skills, and interest in STEM careers. However, it also identifies gaps in the literature related to the development of research attitudes and competencies in high school students, underscoring the need for further research. A substantial portion of the chapter focuses on multidisciplinary research experiences, with a particular emphasis on the Chemistry-Based High School Research Experience (CHSRE) program. This program is highlighted as a model for implementing RCT, showcasing how multidisciplinary research not only develops students' research skills but also cultivates a growth mindset and resilience, which are essential for long-term commitment to STEM careers. The chapter concludes by discussing the role of near-peer mentoring in supporting cognitive and social development within research settings. It reviews evidence showing that near-peer mentoring positively impacts mentees' academic and social outcomes. Overall, this chapter provides a comprehensive overview of how dynamic, real-world research experiences can revolutionize RCT, equipping pre-university students for successful academic and professional paths in research-intensive fields.

Keywords Multidisciplinary Research · Near-Peer Mentoring Model · Research Cognitive Behavior · Experiential Learning · Instructional Design

4.1 Theory of Revolutionizing RCT Through Dynamic Real-World Experiential Research for Pre-University Students

The late 20th century witnessed the engagement of different universities and industries, involving high school students in research laboratories during summer vacations as apprentices. These programs were successful in adapting the k-12 learning experience to a real-world research environment. Students worked in laboratories engaging in hands-on experience as apprentices to scientists who were conducting scientific research, however, neither the nature of these activities nor its effectiveness were hardly documented (Bleicher, 1996). The take-aways from these programs were later studied in the pre-text of remodelling school education thereafter leading to the upgradation of laboratory-based learning at schools (Roth & Roychoudhury, 1993). Diverse studies have proven that learning in a research-based education environment can prompt high school students to become more independent, autonomous, and critical learners. The scope of multidisciplinary learning through research enables them to succeed and grooms them to adapt to changing employment requirements and career shifts (Jackson & Ward, 2004). These challenging settings carry out activities where learners conduct research for exploring knowledge would test them to encounter diverse conditions and enhance their problem-solving skills (Anning, 1994; Jonassen et al., 2006; Woods et al., 1997). Later, laboratory-based research activities embedded within the curriculum that subjected students to scientific research were carried out as teaching interventions to attract the students to learn science. A wealth of empirical studies has unequivocally demonstrated that involving secondary school students in genuine research initiatives, ones that address real-world challenges and facilitate a profound comprehension of scientific principles, enhances the likelihood of these students opting for and sustaining careers in science (Burgin et al., 2012; Kitchen et al., 2018; Roberts & Wassersug, 2009; Sadler et al., 2010; Sasson, 2019; Tai et al., 2017). Consequently, Research-based learning (RBL) was introduced to the school curriculum to create an effective approach to enhance students' learning in STEM disciplines. Despite of the advantages of authentic student research, such as cultivating open-ended inquiry, forging interdisciplinary connections, and enhancing skill sets, there is substantial evidence to suggest that secondary school students who participate in RBL activities experienced significant growth in their research capabilities, as well as an improved understanding of the essence of scientific inquiry and the development of scientific skills (Aydeniz et al., 2011; Charney et al., 2007; Eales, 2014; Eales & Laksana, 2016). Scientific research experiences opened a myriad of possibilities for creative exploration, higher thinking, innovation, and imagination, as they engaged learners in complex and dynamic environments that required hands-on experience. As in the case of social science disciplines, research-based activities were carried out as field trips to perform social experiments and or internet-based research. Internet-based research was quite widely practiced with the onset of the digital era, whereby students engage in learning from different sources of information from which some may be unreliable with lack of depth or clarity (Ellis et al., 2011).

Meanwhile, in the past couple of decades, there has been a gradual shift in RBL being employed at the secondary education levels (Abdelrahman & Yilmaz, 2012; Danch, 2019). There exists a broad consensus within educational circles that fostering the acquisition of 21st-century skills among secondary school students through immersive STEM programs is of paramount importance (Puslednik & Brennan, 2020). This is because high school serves as an opportune moment to introduce students to RBL, enabling them to cultivate a deeper understanding of various subjects and honing their personal and social skills through collaborative and independent research endeavours. These research experiences play a pivotal role in fostering students' intellectual and professional development, enhancing their conceptual knowledge, and instilling a mindset centred around scientific thinking. Through RBL, students embark on a journey of exploration into their interests and gain exposure to potential career opportunities in research-oriented fields (Guillen et al., 2011). Furthermore, implementing RBL during pre-university years has been shown to significantly enhance students' research self-efficacy. These experiences contribute to an increase in students' interest and confidence in conducting research during their college years (Swan et al., 2018; Tai et al., 2006). Thus, RBL can not only enrich high school students' educational experiences but also lay a strong foundation for their future academic and professional pursuits in research and related fields.

Nevertheless, the effective implementation of such programs necessitates a substantial degree of transformation encompassing all echelons of the education system, including the national, state, and regional levels. Effecting the requisite changes for the successful execution of these programs can also pose a formidable challenge for educational systems (Ritz & Fan, 2015). Moreover, educators emphasize the significance of social contexts as a predictor of student learning (Tai et al., 2006). Specifically, the degree to which a research experience is seamlessly integrated into a school's culture and curriculum is deemed crucial. Given all these considerations, there is a pressing need to develop innovative, theoretically sound, empirically proven, and effective high school pedagogical approaches that incorporate the principles of RBL.

Though the research was practiced by high school students through independent as well as integrated RL and different research skills developed were reported, none of the aforementioned studies offered insights into the students' cognitive behaviour development. Research attitudes or competencies were hardly discussed in the studies mentioned previously, with the articles focusing on subject interest and subject productivity as the desired outcome. This was later studied by our research team by carrying out a multidisciplinary research experience program that focused on fostering their research attitudes and competencies. A research experience model was also conceptualized, which will be later explained in the upcoming sections. Another limitation of the apprenticeship model and RBL-focused studies was that learner outcomes were studied from the perspective of hands-on experience or experiential learning. Similar studies did not project the learner attitude development and hence the role of social context or the learning environment was not deeply dissected for a deeper understanding. As there is a lack of literature that emphasizes on research cognitive behaviour in high school context, we will be validating the proposed theory based on our research experiences and conceptualized models.

The following subsections in this chapter outline strategies designed to revolutionize RCT through real-world experiential research opportunities for pre-university students.

4.2 Multidisciplinary Research Experience and Research Cognitive Behavior

4.2.1 Why a Dynamic Multidisciplinary Research Experience?

Currently the educational community is confronted with novel challenges that demand acknowledging the students on the existence of interrelationships and applications of multiple disciplines in ways previously unexplored. There is a growing consensus that scientists must alter both the nature of the problems they engage with and the methodologies they employ to tackle these issues (Lubchenco, 1998; Palmer et al., 2005) depending upon the demands and the severity. Present-day critical global issues such as climate change, the quality of water and air, loss of biodiversity, sustainable global energy consumption, and the emergence, reemergence, and spread of diseases are intricate and intricately interwoven with social and political dimensions. Consequently, they defy resolution within the confines of a single discipline (Palmer et al., 2005). Also, while traditional integrated educational approaches like STEM provide a fundamental groundwork that is indispensable for fostering a deep comprehension of the core principles within each respective discipline, the scope of contemporary challenges that must be confronted to attain a sustainable society necessitates a holistic integration of all the facets of sustainability science. This encompasses research into biological systems, technological systems, geophysical systems, and social systems, along with the forging of robust collaborations with computer science and mathematics.

College educators have traditionally grappled with the delicate balance between the need for students to acquire both a broad understanding and a deep expertise within their chosen fields of study. This pedagogical approach has often leaned toward discipline-based learning, where students immerse themselves in the intricacies of a specific subject. However, as society confronts increasingly intricate and multifaceted challenges that demand holistic, systems-thinking solutions, the significance of cultivating professionals who possess the capability to collaborate across diverse disciplines has surged. In broad terms, addressing this new educational imperative can be pursued through one of two avenues:

(1) Interdisciplinary Approach: This methodology entails the fusion of concepts from various disciplines to engender novel modes of thinking. Participants in such endeavors are required to attain proficiency in the relevant disciplines to facilitate the generation of innovative approaches.
(2) Multidisciplinary Approach: In this approach, the unique viewpoints and principles of each discipline are harnessed to address specific facets of a complex problem. Unlike the interdisciplinary approach, fluency in all the participating disciplines is not obligatory, as the focus is on utilizing the distinct strengths of each discipline to tackle particular dimensions of the challenge at hand.

The crux of the matter lies in ensuring that every participant comprehends the multifaceted nature of the problem at hand and possesses the essential skills for effective communication. This communication is the linchpin for collaborative problem-solving, achieved through a shared perspective (Rogers et al., 2015). While it is true that numerous substantial sustainability challenges may necessitate an interdisciplinary approach, the project developers contend that a multidisciplinary approach to scientific education holds immense merit. Firstly, a strictly interdisciplinary approach often demands a restructuring of the conventional boundaries that delineate academic disciplines, potentially entailing substantial financial and administrative support. Conversely, a multidisciplinary approach harmonizes well with the existing structures prevalent in contemporary higher education institutions. Secondly, the project developers assert that emphasizing a multidisciplinary perspective is a vital precursor to nurturing individuals who can eventually evolve into adept interdisciplinary problem solvers (Remington-Doucette et al., 2013).

4.2.2 *Multidisciplinary Chemistry-Based High School Research Experience (CHSRE) Program Implementing the Research Cognitive Theory*

An empirically established method to develop high school student's research attitudes and competencies is through subjecting dynamic multidisciplinary research experiences (Ahmad et al., 2021; Bell, 2011; Burgin et al., 2012; Kettler & Puryear, 2021; Robnett et al., 2015; Schwartz & Crawford, 2006) that leads the theoretical proposal on the RCT. RCT can be established through our study that implemented an innovative multidisciplinary chemistry-based high school research experience (CHSRE) program using chemistry-centric research projects to enhance high school students' research capabilities and attitudes (Al-Thani et al., 2022). The research employed a mixed-methods approach, involving an indirect assessment of program effectiveness, surveys administered to students, research assistants, and the research faculty mentors engaged in the program. Another key highlight of the study revealed that the implementation of the multidisciplinary model also helped to retain high school students' interest in STEM careers. Also, such a dynamic learning environment proved to promote high school students to join STEM majors in undergraduate courses, and further aspire for STEM careers (Remington-Doucette et al., 2013).

The study demonstrated that multidisciplinary research experiences can ignite a deep-seated passion towards the context by showing students the applicability of their research. As students engage in collaborative research projects that draw from various fields, they gain a holistic understanding from their research community of how different discipline concepts are interconnected and applied to address multifaceted challenges. As they engage in literature review on different interdisciplinary topics, they undergo different discussions within their community, which indeed foster a sense of belonging and curiosity. Also, the research environment enclosed multidisciplinary fields helps students to develop their intellectual cognitive abilities as they partake in experimentation, failure, and iterative problem-solving. This helped the students to reproduce the experiments, embedding the conceptual understanding of the subject matter in them. Moreover, such multidisciplinary research experiences proved to encourage students to develop a growth mindset, wherein they become more resilient in the face of challenges and setbacks. This mindset shift can significantly impact their long-term commitment to STEM careers, thereby nurturing extrinsic motivation in them. Through these processes the complete observational process—attention, retention, reproduction, and motivation is achieved to bring desirable behavioral change in the high school students.

Furthermore, exposure to multidisciplinary research can broaden students' horizons regarding potential STEM career paths. They gain insights into the diverse array of roles and professions within STEM, beyond the conventional stereotypes. This exposure helps them make informed decisions about their educational and career trajectories, increasing the likelihood of pursuing STEM careers that align with their interests and strengths. Additionally, the collaborative nature of multidisciplinary research experiences nurtures important interpersonal skills, such as effective communication, teamwork, and adaptability. These skills are not only vital for success in STEM careers but also for thriving in an increasingly interconnected global workforce. As students develop these skills during their research endeavors, they are better equipped to excel in their chosen STEM fields and to contribute meaningfully to scientific advancements and innovations. In the long term, the impact of multidisciplinary research experiences on students' attitudes towards STEM careers extends beyond their individual journeys. It can have a ripple effect, as these students may serve as role models, mentors, or advocates for STEM education and careers in their communities. They may inspire future generations to pursue STEM fields, contributing to a more diverse and inclusive STEM workforce that harnesses the full spectrum of human talent and perspectives to tackle the complex challenges facing society. In this way, the integration of multidisciplinary research experiences into education can have far-reaching and transformative effects on students' attitudes, careers, and the broader STEM landscape.

4.2.3 *Instructional Design of the CHSRE Model*

This section describes in detail the instructional design of the multidisciplinary chemistry-based high school research experience (CHSRE) program discussed in Chapter 1.6. While previous research has demonstrated the effectiveness of interdisciplinary approaches, such as combining biology and history, to implement research-based learning (RBL) and enhance high school students' comprehension in specific contexts (Jones et al., 2010; Meerah & Arsad, 2010), our study focused on utilizing chemistry as the core discipline. Chemistry was chosen due to its widespread application in research and its utilization by various educators in research practices (Blonder & Sakhnini, 2017; Shang, 2021). Chemistry plays a pivotal role in multidisciplinary projects by offering a rich tapestry of research opportunities for aspiring scholars. It provides fertile ground for hands-on experience through laboratory-based activities, thereby fostering positive attitudes among students toward the field. Furthermore, chemistry seamlessly integrates with other disciplines, propelling forward multidisciplinary research endeavors. For instance, consider a chemistry-based interdisciplinary project focused on "biodiesel fuel production." In this project, two fundamental concepts from biology (biochemistry of algae) and chemistry (transesterification) were intricately woven together. Through this integrative approach, students not only deepened their understanding but also developed a heightened enthusiasm for research-oriented careers in the realm of algal technology (Levine et al., 2021). Similarly, in another study involving polymeric nanocomposite coatings, various STEM disciplines, including mathematics, chemistry, physics, and technology, were integrated. This interdisciplinary approach encouraged students to explore diverse domains within material science, such as polymers, corrosion, composites, and more (Mansfeld et al., 1998). Projects of this nature equip young scholars with the skills to prepare chemical solutions, conduct material analyses, and achieve enhanced learning outcomes and attitudes in interdisciplinary STEM domains (Al-Thani et al., 2022).

Therefore, the implementation of the CHSRE (see Figure 4.1) proved to be highly effective in bridging the gap between students and the fundamental principles of chemistry, as well as their integration with other disciplines such as material science, engineering, mathematics, and technology, all within the context of real-world applications. Consequently, students actively engaged in scientific experiments that not only bolstered their research competencies but also cultivated positive attitudes toward research endeavors. The primary objective of the study was to explore the extensive potential of multidisciplinary research topics in the realm of chemistry, which provided a fertile environment for nurturing research proficiency and dispositions. The CHSRE model facilitated high school students' access to authentic research laboratories in the domain of chemistry, enabling them to collaborate with research faculty in an environment conducive to genuine research practices. This approach not only led to the development of students' research competencies but also equipped them with the 21st-century skills essential for laboratory work.

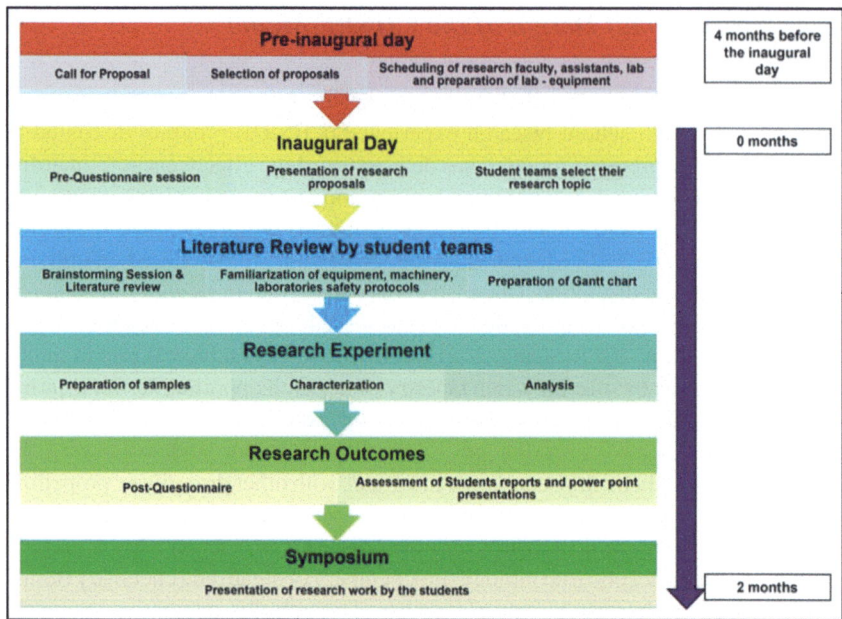

Fig. 4.1 Schematics for the CHSRE Program Methodology. This figure outlines the methodological framework of the Chemistry-Based High School Research Experience (CHSRE) program. It highlights the integration of multidisciplinary research fields and the step-by-step approach to developing research competencies in high school students. Reproduced with permission from (Al-Thani et al., 2022). Copyright American Chemical Society, 2022

4.3 Near Peer Mentoring Model in a Dynamic High School Research Environment

4.3.1 Why the Near Peer Mentoring Model?

In the current era of online education, it is imperative to explore innovative approaches to STEM education that can both inspire and sustain the curiosity of young learners—which is important to develop an intrinsic motivation. One such approach is STEM education facilitated through an online near-peer mentoring model. Traditional mentoring encompasses a hierarchical dynamic, with a younger mentee seeking guidance and wisdom from an elder, experienced mentor. However, it's crucial to recognize that mentoring can take various forms, including a peer or near-peer model where the mentor is of similar age or position to the mentee. This approach, known as near-peer mentorship, holds significant importance for individual development in terms of cognitive, emotional, and behavioral growth. In the context of STEM-based mentoring models, numerous studies have already underscored the benefits of mentoring in fostering these gains (Pluth et al., 2015; Sharpe et al., 2018). Additionally, mentoring in the field of science plays a pivotal role in nurturing early-career scientists (Thiry & Laursen, 2011). In comparison to the traditional model featuring senior mentors, "peer or near-peer mentors" are often deemed more effective due to their relatable experiences, capacity to offer emotional support, and shared personal connections (Parker et al., 2008). The near-peer mentorship model originated at the Walter Reed Army Institute of Research (Jett et al., 2005), where near-peer mentors, typically undergraduate or post-baccalaureate students, guide middle and high school students as part of a summer internship program.

It's worth noting the distinct difference between a classical undergraduate mentoring model and an undergraduate near-peer mentoring model. The former usually involves an undergraduate mentee and an expert mentor (Dolan & Johnson, 2009), with the undergraduate mentee primarily benefiting from the mentor's teaching experience (Landrum & Nelsen, 2002). In contrast, the latter allows the undergraduate mentor to both learn and share knowledge with younger mentees under the guidance of an expert. In the near-peer mentoring model, the crucial determinant of the mentoring relationship is often social and cognitive relatedness (Garcia-Melgar & Meyers, 2020; Ten Cate & Durning, 2007). A study conducted by Goldner L. and Mayseless O. (2009) demonstrated a significant link between the quality of the mentor-mentee relationship and improvements in mentees' academic and social outcomes (Goldner & Mayseless, 2009). Dubois and Neville (1997) further revealed that near-peer mentoring yields enhanced benefits for teenagers (DuBois & Neville, 1997). Specifically, Rhodes et al. (2006) highlighted that high-quality mentoring relationships are characterized by attributes such as closeness between mentor and mentee, the sense of legitimacy, empathy, and empowerment (Rhodes et al., 2005). Moreover, the quality of such mentoring relationships hinges on factors such as the frequency of interactions between the mentor and mentee, the emotional connection they share, and the durability of their relationship (DuBois et al., 2002).

In an educational context, near-peer mentoring involves mentors who are capable of supporting the academic and psychosocial needs of their mentees (Ward et al., 2014). To achieve this, mentors and mentees should share cognitive and social compatibilities or similarities (Ten Cate & Durning, 2007). Social compatibility encompasses perceived social congruences, such as shared educational experiences between mentors and mentees. Such shared experiences foster the development of compassion, trust, confidence, and the willingness to disclose personal thoughts and challenges (Dioso-Henson, 2012). Ten Cate and Durning (2007) associate social congruence with the affective and motivational aspects of learning, asserting that near-peer mentors are often better at understanding students' motivations compared to academic staff (Ten Cate & Durning, 2007). A strong sense of social congruence is established when mentors draw upon their own past or current learning experiences and challenges, enabling mentees to feel understood and facilitating the disclosure of learning gaps. This, in turn, allows mentors to offer targeted support (Lockspeiser et al., 2008), which induces a sense of belonging for the mentees, and thus helping to solidify their intrinsic motivation for the subject matter. In contrast, cognitive similarity refers to mentors' ability to comprehend mentees' cognitive aspects, including their learning processes and challenges (Ten Cate et al., 2012). Cognitive compatibility emerges when mentors can identify mentees' learning gaps and provide guidance and communication tailored to the mentees' current cognitive development (Rhodes et al., 2006). A successful mentoring relationship hinges on both social and cognitive compatibility (Garcia-Melgar & Meyers, 2020), although social compatibility typically forms before cognitive compatibility. An emotional and dynamic connection must first be established before mentors can effectively convey learning objectives to students (Schwartzman, 2013). Therefore, it is essential to develop social compatibility before mentors can leverage their cognitive compatibility to provide academic and motivational support. The establishment of such compatibility, encompassing both social and cognitive congruence, in an online setting warrants in-depth exploration, especially when developing online near-peer mentoring models for STEM education. In our study (Al-Thani et al., 2023), we designed and implemented a STEM-based online near-peer mentoring approach for high school students (see Figure 4.2). One noteworthy finding from our investigation was that the dynamic research environment increased the mentee's retention, engagement, and motivation—closely satisfying the attention, retention, reproduction, and motivation process. Such a model proved to ensure the curiosity of students to be intact and attract students towards STEM disciplines and opportunities. Consequently, emphasizing the motivational aspect of online near-peer mentoring in STEM education is particularly critical, as a lack of motivation and engagement is widely recognized as one of the most challenging aspects of online education (DeCoito & Estaiteyeh, 2022). Therefore, through the near-peer learning model, by focusing on motivation, we can enhance student engagement and promote self-regulated learning.

4.4 Learning Through "Research Cognitive Theory" for High School Research Experiences

Research Experience Programs (REPs) are a valuable way to introduce students to the field of scientific research (Feldman et al., 2009). At their core, REPs provide students with an understanding of research methodology, which enhances their comprehension of scientific knowledge (Leedy & Ormrod, 2005). These programs foster the development of essential research skills in students, such as critical thinking, problem-solving, analysis, and the ability to communicate findings. Traditionally, REPs have been primarily offered at the university level; however, there has been a noticeable trend in recent decades to introduce them at the secondary and elementary school levels (Abdelrahman & Yilmaz, 2012; Danch, 2019). High school, in particular, is an ideal time to immerse students in REPs, providing them with a deeper understanding of academic subjects and encouraging both collaborative and independent research endeavors. High School Research Experience Programs (HSREPs) serve as a platform for enhancing students' intellectual and professional development through the exploration of concepts and practical scientific experience. As a result,

4.4 Learning Through "Research Cognitive Theory" for High School …

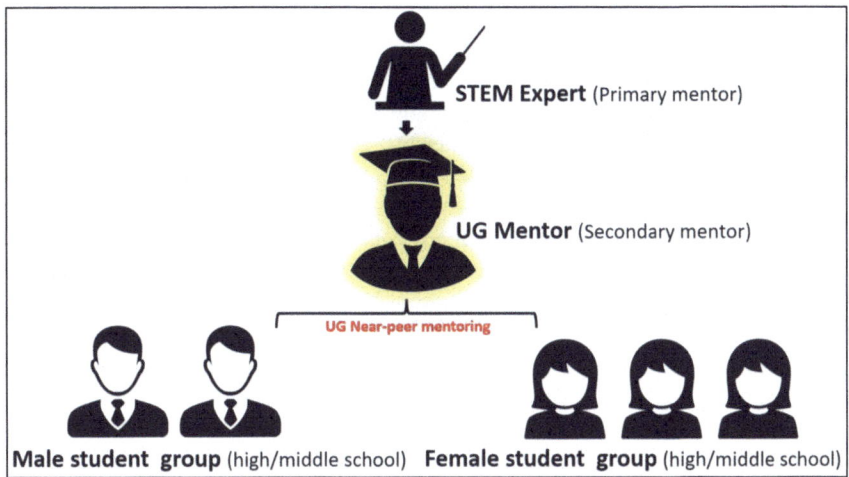

Fig. 4.2 Hierarchy of the Mentoring Model. This figure illustrates the structure of the near-peer mentoring model, highlighting the relationship between undergraduate mentors and student mentees within a dynamic research environment. It emphasizes the collaborative framework fostering guidance, social connection, and skill development. Reproduced with permission licensed under CC BY 4.0 (Al-Thani et al., 2023)

students engage in research activities based on their interests and gain exposure to potential career paths in research-oriented fields (Guillen et al., 2011). Moreover, pre-college research experiences help foster research self-efficacy in students, which boosts their motivation and confidence to conduct research in college (Swan et al., 2018; Tai et al., 2006).

When students participate in research experiences, they become familiar with the inquiry process, sharpen their problem-solving skills, understand data collection techniques, and learn to draw meaningful conclusions from their research. The inquiry process embodies the practices, conceptual needs, and values associated with "authentic science" (Sadler et al., 2010). However, it is important to recognize that REPs are not standardized globally, and research has shown variations in how these programs are implemented (Abd-El-Khalick et al., 2004; Hofstein et al., 2005). For example, while inquiry-based education often incorporates hands-on activities, it may not always focus on the intellectual engagement or "minds-on" aspects. The absence of clearly defined goals in the inquiry process can undermine the authenticity of the research experience (RE). Additionally, the emphasis on high-stakes standardized testing has shifted attention away from lab-based investigations. In response, efforts have been made to integrate real research methodologies into secondary education, aiming to engage students in more effective, knowledge-based learning (King et al., 2008; Neber & Anton, 2008). Notable initiatives include Australian educators creating specialized chemistry contexts that give students greater autonomy and extended time for experiments. In Germany, pre-experiment activities enable students to select and design their own research projects. Furthermore, the national curriculum in the United Kingdom stresses the importance of research exploration in school science subjects.

Although educators are working to provide research experiences for high school students, there is a notable gap in developing a replicable, theoretically grounded, and empirically validated learning framework for imparting research experiences in schools (Bergmann et al., 2021; Meerah & Arsad, 2010; Sabirova & Zakirova, 2015). This is crucial because navigating the research process independently presents various challenges, such as balancing focus between both the final product and the learning process, as well as developing critical skills and overcoming common obstacles. A key aspect of this process is the learning framework, which plays a crucial role in guiding students through these challenges. Moreover, while high school educators are generally knowledgeable in their subject areas, they often lack experience in mentoring high school students through research processes, which can limit their effectiveness as guides. Additionally, due to their limited scientific background and more restrictive schedules compared to university students, high school students require a robust learning framework to navigate these challenges effectively. To address these obstacles and maximize the value of research experiences, it is essential to develop a learning framework that is theoretically sound and that improves teaching practices in both school and research settings.

High School Research Experience Programs (HSREPs) require a research-based learning framework to cultivate intrinsic motivation, self-efficacy, and intellectual growth. Engaging high school students in authentic learning processes is crucial, not just in terms of knowledge acquisition but also in providing them with deep engagement with the scientific method. Thus, the theoretical foundation of this study is grounded in Research Cognitive Theory (RCT), which suggests that intellectual learning occurs within a dynamic research environment and as a result of the reciprocal interaction between the individual, their environment, and their behavior (as shown in Fig. 1.6). The distinctiveness of RCT lies in its focus on the influence of a dynamic research environment and its emphasis on intrinsic intellectual reinforcement. Research experiences shape an individual's prospects, beliefs, and reinforcements, all of which influence their engagement in intellectual learning. RCT highlights the role of individual research practices in shaping intrinsic motivation and the factors that influence intellectual behavior. Additionally, the theory provides intellectual support by fostering expectations, self-efficacy, and leveraging research learning and other reinforcements to bring about behavioral change. In summary, RCT emphasizes the role of research activities in influencing intellectual behavior, in contrast to Social Cognitive Theory (SCT), which stresses the mental processes involved in shaping behavior, and Social Learning Theory (SLT), which focuses on the role of observation and imitation in learning (Al-Thani & Ahmad, 2025).

The High School Research Cognitive Learning Program (HSRCLP) was designed to offer students a dynamic research learning environment (publication under review at Heliyon) rooted in the theoretical foundations of Social Learning Theory (SLT) and Social Cognitive Theory (SCT) (Al-Thani & Ahmad, 2025). The learning process is initiated through the steps of attention, retention, reproduction, and motivation. Activities within the program are carefully structured to capture students' attention,

4.4 Learning Through "Research Cognitive Theory" for High School ...

ensuring they are actively engaged with the content. Retention is maintained through brainstorming sessions that prompt students to explore the topic more deeply and form meaningful connections with the concepts being learned. The program then provides students with hands-on, experimental activities that allow them to apply and solidify their understanding of the material through practice. To sustain motivation throughout the learning process, positive reinforcements such as prizes, competitions, and national-level recognition are incorporated.

Each step of this learning process—attention, retention, motivation, and reproduction—is delivered through a pedagogical approach combining challenge-based learning (CBL) with a blended approach of problem-based and project-based learning (PBL + PjBL) (Al-Thani & Ahmad, 2025). CBL serves as the foundation by introducing real-world challenges that stretch beyond students' current knowledge and capabilities, encouraging them to explore multiple possible solutions. This encourages students to think creatively and step outside the box. PBL and PjBL further build on this by posing a driving question that guides student inquiry and research. Additionally, PjBL's emphasis on hands-on learning reinforces the understanding of concepts through experimental activities, allowing students to apply the knowledge they have gained. The framework for the model is shown in Fig. 4.3.

It is important to note that SLT plays a pivotal role in the program by fostering observational learning, where students observe and imitate the research behaviors of both mentors and peers, thus helping them internalize research skills and develop a scientific identity. Through collaboration with peers and mentorship, students learn by modeling the behaviors of those around them, aligning with SLT's principles of learning through observation and interaction. Simultaneously, SCT's focus on self-efficacy, self-regulation, and reciprocal determinism is reflected in the program's structure. The program actively cultivates research self-efficacy by providing students with opportunities to engage in hands-on research tasks, receiving mentorship feedback, and creating a supportive learning environment. This boosts students' confidence in their ability to succeed in scientific inquiry, aligning with SCT's emphasis on personal agency and cognitive development. The steps of attention, retention, reproduction, and motivation directly tie into SCT's framework, as they involve cognitive tasks that promote deeper learning and strengthen self-efficacy. By integrating both theories, the program enhances students' research attitudes, scientific identity, and cognitive abilities, aiming to foster 21st-century research competencies. This synergy of SLT and SCT effectively supports the program's objectives by enhancing students' research behaviors and attitudes, facilitating cognitive growth, and encouraging behavioral change in an interactive and supportive environment.

This dynamic research learning environment exemplifies the triadic reciprocal causation in SCT, where behavioral, cognitive, and environmental factors interact. In the HSRCLP, students' behavioral factors are demonstrated by their direct engagement in research tasks and by observing successful outcomes, which in turn strengthen their 21st-century skills and self-efficacy. Their cognitive or personal factors are shaped by their attitudes, beliefs, and motivation as they engage with the dynamic research environment. Finally, the environmental factors are purposefully crafted to be interactive and supportive, where students interact with their peers,

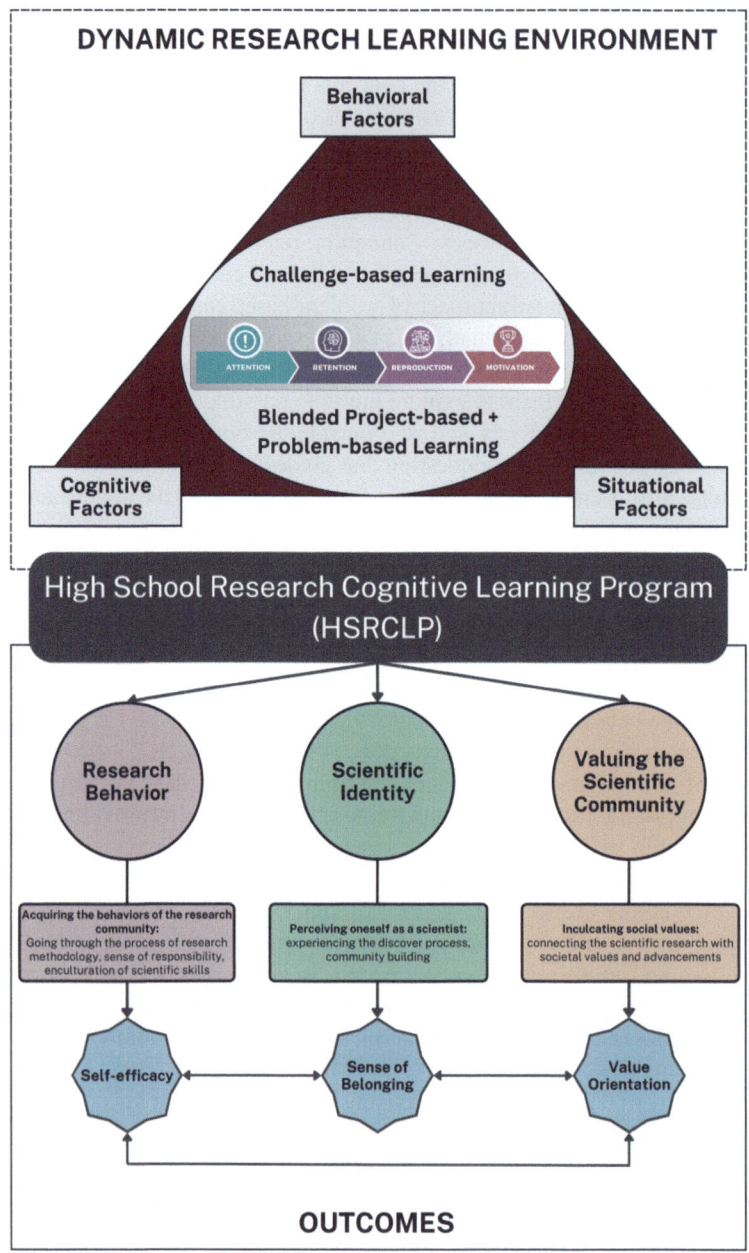

Fig. 4.3 The High School Research Cognitive Learning Program (HSRCLP). This figure represents the structured framework of HSRCLP, integrating Challenge-Based Learning (CBL) with a blended Problem-Based and Project-Based Learning (PBL + PjBL) approach. It highlights the program's steps—attention, retention, reproduction, and motivation—designed to foster research attitudes, self-efficacy, and cognitive growth among high school students. Reproduced with permission licensed under CC BY 4.0 (Al-Thani & Ahmad, 2025)

mentors, and research projects, thereby illustrating the influence of the environment on their learning experience.

By employing a comprehensive approach grounded in Social Learning Theory (SLT) and Social Cognitive Theory (SCT) and utilizing pedagogical strategies based on Challenge-Based Learning (CBL) and a blended PBL+PjBL framework, the findings from this study demonstrate that the program successfully nurtures essential research attitudes in high school students. The proposed intervention has shown greater effectiveness compared to traditional research programs in promoting positive research behaviors, fostering a strong scientific identity, and instilling a sense of value for the scientific community. These outcomes reflect the integration of 21st-century skills among students. As such, the study makes significant contributions to both educational research and practice by presenting a tangible, scalable framework that bridges the gap between theoretical foundations and practical application in secondary education research programs. It offers a replicable model designed to cultivate research attitudes, enhance critical thinking, and encourage engagement in STEM fields, equipping educators to better prepare students for future careers in science. Future research should focus on conducting longitudinal studies to evaluate the long-term effects of the High School Research Cognitive Learning Program (HSRCLP) on student performance, sustained scientific engagement, and career pathways. Additionally, using mixed-method approaches, including qualitative data, would provide more in-depth insights into student experiences and the influence of mentor-student interactions. Educational policymakers are encouraged to consider integrating research-driven frameworks like the HSRCLP into national curricula, particularly in STEM education. Ensuring adequate funding and resources to scale these programs across various educational contexts can facilitate broader implementation and support the development of the next generation of researchers and innovators.

4.5 Chapter Summary

In this chapter, we discuss to revolutionize Research Cognitive Theory (RCT) through transformative research experiences in high schools. These experiences draw from real-world applications, immersing students in authentic research tasks that bridge the gap between theoretical knowledge and practical exploration. High school marks a crucial phase for introducing Research-Based Learning (RBL), fostering critical thinking, problem-solving, and collaborative abilities while nurturing an appreciation for STEM careers. By participating in multidisciplinary research, students gain intellectual autonomy and practical insights into complex global issues. Early research apprenticeship models, though beneficial, often lacked documentation on their impact on cognitive development and attitudes, prompting the development of newer, dynamic RBL frameworks aimed at enhancing both research skills and scientific mindsets.

The chapter delves deeper into a dynamic multidisciplinary approach, using chemistry as a core discipline to foster integration with other fields like biology, engineering, and technology. Programs like the Chemistry-Based High School Research Experience (CHSRE) emphasize hands-on research to build student competencies while simultaneously nurturing curiosity and a growth mindset. These multidisciplinary experiences help students form connections between different domains, promoting critical collaboration and adaptability. Additionally, the chapter discusses the transformative role of near-peer mentoring models, wherein mentors closer in age to mentees provide relatable guidance, fostering trust, cognitive alignment, and emotional engagement. Such models have proven effective in sustaining motivation and interest in STEM, even within online learning environments, as they promote a sense of belonging and self-efficacy among students.

A significant highlight is the introduction of the High School Research Cognitive Learning Program (HSRCLP), a structured framework integrating Challenge-Based Learning (CBL) and a blended Problem-Based and Project-Based Learning (PBL + PjBL) approach. This model combines observational learning with mentorship, leveraging both Social Learning Theory (SLT) and Social Cognitive Theory (SCT). By aligning cognitive tasks with real-world challenges, the program fosters critical skills, intrinsic motivation, and scientific identity. The chapter emphasizes the scalability of this model and its potential to address current gaps in research education. It calls for continued exploration of its long-term impact on student outcomes and integration into broader educational policies to cultivate the next generation of innovative thinkers and researchers.

Glossary

Term	Definition
Research Cognitive Theory (RCT)	A theoretical framework emphasizing the role of research environments and practices in shaping cognitive and intellectual development
Research-Based Learning (RBL)	An educational approach where students engage in authentic research activities to enhance understanding, skills, and critical thinking
21st-Century Skills	Competencies like critical thinking, collaboration, problem-solving, and digital literacy essential for modern careers
Multidisciplinary Approach	A method of addressing problems by integrating knowledge and perspectives from multiple disciplines while maintaining their unique contributions

(continued)

Glossary

(continued)

Term	Definition
Interdisciplinary Approach	A method that fuses concepts from various disciplines to create new ways of thinking and solving problems
Chemistry-Based High School Research Experience (CHSRE)	A program that uses chemistry as a core discipline to foster multidisciplinary learning and research skills among high school students
Growth Mindset	A belief in the ability to develop skills and intelligence through effort, learning from challenges and setbacks
Near-Peer Mentoring	A mentorship model where mentors are of a similar age or position as mentees, fostering relatability and shared experiences
Social Learning Theory (SLT)	A theory emphasizing learning through observation, imitation, and interaction with others
Social Cognitive Theory (SCT)	A theory focusing on the interplay between personal factors, behaviors, and environmental influences in shaping learning
High School Research Cognitive Learning Program (HSRCLP)	A structured research education program integrating CBL, PBL, and PjBL, grounded in SLT and SCT, designed for high school students
Challenge-Based Learning (CBL)	An educational approach where students solve real-world challenges by exploring multiple solutions and engaging in active inquiry
Problem-Based Learning (PBL)	A student-centered approach that involves learning through solving open-ended problems and applying critical thinking
Project-Based Learning (PjBL)	A teaching method where students work on extended projects to create tangible outcomes, promoting hands-on and collaborative learning
Research Experience Program (REP)	Programs that immerse students in authentic research practices to develop inquiry, critical thinking, and problem-solving skills
Research Self-Efficacy	Confidence in one's ability to conduct research effectively, often developed through hands-on experiences and mentorship
Minds-On Learning	An approach emphasizing intellectual engagement and critical thinking alongside hands-on activities
Triadic Reciprocal Causation	A concept from SCT describing the dynamic interaction between behavior, cognition, and environmental factors in learning
Intrinsic Motivation	Internal drive to engage in activities for personal satisfaction and growth rather than external rewards

(continued)

(continued)

Term	Definition
STEM Careers	Careers in Science, Technology, Engineering, and Mathematics, often requiring critical thinking, problem-solving, and innovation skills
Dynamic Research Environment	A setting that combines hands-on experimentation, collaboration, and mentorship to foster active learning and critical skills

References

Abd-El-Khalick, F., Boujaoude, S., Duschl, R., Lederman, N. G., Mamlok-Naaman, R., Hofstein, A., Niaz, M., Treagust, D., & Tuan, H. (2004). Inquiry in science education: International perspectives. *Science Education, 88*(3), 397–419. https://doi.org/10.1002/sce.10118

Abdelrahman, M., & Yilmaz, M. (2012). Best practices in creating and running research experience programs. In *2012 ASEE Annual Conference & Exposition.*

Ahmad, Z., Ammar, M., & Al-Thani, N. J. (2021). Pedagogical models to implement effective stem research experience programs in high school students. *Education Sciences, 11*(11), 743.

Al-Thani, N. J., & Ahmad, Z. (2025). Learning through "research cognitive theory": A new framework for developing 21st century research skills in secondary school students. *Heliyon.*

Al-Thani, N. J., Saad, A., Siby, N., Bhadra, J., & Ahmad, Z. (2022). The role of multidisciplinary chemistry informal research programs in building research competencies and attitudes. *Journal of Chemical Education, 99*(5), 1957–1970.

Al-Thani, N. J., Santhosh, M. E., Bhadra, J., & Ahmad, Z. (2023). The prominent roles of undergraduate mentors in an online near-peer mentoring model. *Sustainability, 15*(4), 3020.

Anning, A. (1994). Dilemmas and opportunities of a new curriculum: Design and technology with young children. *International Journal of Technology and Design Education, 4*, 155–177.

Aydeniz, M., Baksa, K., & Skinner, J. (2011). Understanding the impact of an apprenticeship-based scientific research program on high school students' understanding of scientific inquiry. *Journal of Science Education and Technology, 20*, 403–421.

Bell, E. (2011). Research experiences for high school students.

Bergmann, M., Schäpke, N., Marg, O., Stelzer, F., Lang, D. J., Bossert, M., Gantert, M., Häußler, E., Marquardt, E., & Piontek, F. M. (2021). Transdisciplinary sustainability research in real-world labs: Success factors and methods for change. *Sustainability Science, 16*, 541–564.

Bleicher, R. E. (1996). High school students learning science in university research laboratories. *Journal of Research in Science Teaching, 33*(10), 1115–1133. https://doi.org/10.1002/(SICI)1098-2736(199612)33:10%3c1115::AID-TEA5%3e3.0.CO;2-V

Blonder, R., & Sakhnini, S. (2017). Finding the connections between a high-school chemistry curriculum and nano-scale science and technology. *Chemistry Education Research and Practice, 18*(4), 903–922.

Burgin, S. R., Sadler, T. D., & Koroly, M. J. (2012). High school student participation in scientific research apprenticeships: Variation in and relationships among student experiences and outcomes. *Research in Science Education, 42*, 439–467.

Charney, J., Hmelo-Silver, C. E., Sofer, W., Neigeborn, L., Coletta, S., & Nemeroff, M. (2007). Cognitive apprenticeship in science through immersion in laboratory practices. *International Journal of Science Education, 29*(2), 195–213.

Danch, J. M. (2019). The impact of a high school research course on participants at the undergraduate, graduate and post-graduate levels. AGU Fall Meeting Abstracts,

References

DeCoito, I., & Estaiteyeh, M. (2022). Transitioning to online teaching during the COVID-19 pandemic: An exploration of STEM teachers' views, successes, and challenges. *Journal of Science Education and Technology, 31*(3), 340–356.

Dioso-Henson, L. (2012). The effect of reciprocal peer tutoring and non-reciprocal peer tutoring on the performance of students in college physics. *Research in Education, 87*(1), 34–49.

Dolan, E., & Johnson, D. (2009). Toward a holistic view of undergraduate research experiences: An exploratory study of impact on graduate/postdoctoral mentors. *Journal of Science Education and Technology, 18,* 487–500.

DuBois, D. L., Holloway, B. E., Valentine, J. C., & Cooper, H. (2002). Effectiveness of mentoring programs for youth: A meta-analytic review. *American Journal of Community Psychology, 30*(2), 157–197.

DuBois, D. L., & Neville, H. A. (1997). Youth mentoring: Investigation of relationship characteristics and perceived benefits. *Journal of Community Psychology, 25*(3), 227–234.

Eales, J. (2014). *Student research and publishing program in secondary school science: A study of its effects and development of a model for implementation* [PhD dissertation, Assumption University].

Eales, J., & Laksana, S. (2016). Establishing a student research and publishing program in high school physics. *The Physics Teacher, 54*(3), 178–181.

Ellis, R. A., Goodyear, P., Bliuc, A.-M., & Ellis, M. (2011). High school students' experiences of learning through research on the Internet. *Journal of Computer Assisted Learning, 27*(6), 503–515. https://doi.org/10.1111/j.1365-2729.2011.00412.x

Feldman, A., Divoll, K., & Rogan-Klyve, A. (2009). Research education of new scientists: Implications for science teacher education. *Journal of Research in Science Teaching: THe Official Journal of the National Association for Research in Science Teaching, 46*(4), 442–459. https://doi.org/10.1002/tea.20285

Garcia-Melgar, A., & Meyers, N. (2020). STEM near peer mentoring for secondary school students: A case study of university mentors' experiences with online mentoring. *Journal for STEM Education Research, 3,* 19–42.

Goldner, L., & Mayseless, O. (2009). The quality of mentoring relationships and mentoring success. *Journal of Youth and Adolescence, 38,* 1339–1350.

Guillen, T. D., Yilmaz, M., Garcia, C. A., & Ramirez, D. (2011). A K-12 advanced research camp for engineering and science disciplines. In *2011 ASEE Annual Conference & Exposition.*

Hofstein, A., Navon, O., Kipnis, M., & Mamlok-Naaman, R. (2005). Developing students' ability to ask more and better questions resulting from inquiry-type chemistry laboratories. *Journal of Research in Science Teaching, 42*(7), 791–806. https://doi.org/10.1002/tea.20072

Jackson, N., & Ward, R. (2004). A fresh perspective on progress files—A way of representing complex learning and achievement in higher education. *Assessment & Evaluation in Higher Education, 29*(4), 423–449.

Jett, M., Anderson, M., & Yourick, D. (2005). Near peer mentoring: A step-wise means of engaging young students in science. *FASEB Journal.*

Jonassen, D., Strobel, J., & Lee, C. B. (2006). Everyday problem solving in engineering: Lessons for engineering educators. *Journal of Engineering Education, 95*(2), 139–151.

Jones, M. T., Barlow, A. E., & Villarejo, M. (2010). Importance of undergraduate research for minority persistence and achievement in biology. *The Journal of Higher Education, 81*(1), 82–115.

Kettler, T., & Puryear, J. S. (2021). Research experiences for high school students: A curriculum for expertise and authentic practice. In *Modern curriculum for gifted and advanced academic students* (pp. 189–203). Routledge.

King, D., Bellocchi, A., & Ritchie, S. M. (2008). Making connections: Learning and teaching chemistry in context. *Research in Science Education, 38,* 365–384.

Kitchen, J. A., Sonnert, G., & Sadler, P. M. (2018). The impact of college-and university-run high school summer programs on students' end of high school STEM career aspirations. *Science Education, 102*(3), 529–547.

Landrum, R. E., & Nelsen, L. R. (2002). The undergraduate research assistantship: An analysis of the benefits. *Teaching of Psychology, 29*(1), 15–19.

Leedy, P. D., & Ormrod, J. E. (2005). *Practical research* (Vol. 108). Pearson Custom Saddle River, NJ.

Levine, I. A., Gerk, C. L., Gómez, S. M., Nalley, J. O., & Nalley, M. M. (2021). The algae foundation® and algae technology educational consortium. *Journal of the World Aquaculture Society, 52*(5), 1099–1117.

Lockspeiser, T. M., O'Sullivan, P., Teherani, A., & Muller, J. (2008). Understanding the experience of being taught by peers: The value of social and cognitive congruence. *Advances in Health Sciences Education, 13*, 361–372.

Lubchenco, J. (1998). Entering the century of the environment: A new social contract for science. *Science, 279*(5350), 491–497.

Mansfeld, F., Han, L., Lee, C., & Zhang, G. (1998). Evaluation of corrosion protection by polymer coatings using electrochemical impedance spectroscopy and noise analysis. *Electrochimica Acta, 43*(19–20), 2933–2945.

Meerah, T. S. M., & Arsad, N. M. (2010). Developing research skills at secondary school. *Procedia-Social and Behavioral Sciences, 9*, 512–516.

Neber, H., & Anton, M. (2008). Promoting pre-experimental activities in high-school chemistry: Focusing on the role of students' epistemic questions. *International Journal of Science Education, 30*(13), 1801–1821. https://doi.org/10.1080/09500690701579546

Palmer, M. A., Bernhardt, E. S., Chornesky, E. A., Collins, S. L., Dobson, A. P., Duke, C. S., Gold, B. D., Jacobson, R. B., Kingsland, S. E., Kranz, R. H., Mappin, M. J., Martinez, M. L., Micheli, F., Morse, J. L., Pace, M. L., Pascual, M., Palumbi, S. S., Reichman, O., Townsend, A. R., & Turner, M. G. (2005). Ecological science and sustainability for the 21st century. *Frontiers in Ecology and the Environment, 3*(1), 4–11. https://doi.org/10.1890/1540-9295(2005)003[0004:ESASFT]2.0.CO;2

Parker, P., Hall, D. T., & Kram, K. E. (2008). Peer coaching: A relational process for accelerating career learning. *Academy of Management Learning & Education, 7*(4), 487–503.

Pluth, M. D., Boettcher, S. W., Nazin, G. V., Greenaway, A. L., & Hartle, M. D. (2015). Collaboration and near-peer mentoring as a platform for sustainable science education outreach. *Journal of Chemical Education, 92*(4), 625–630.

Puslednik, L., & Brennan, P. C. (2020, August). An Australian-based authentic science research programme transforms the 21st century learning of rural high school students. *Australian Journal of Education, 64*(2), 98–112. https://doi.org/10.1177/0004944120919890

Remington-Doucette, S. M., Hiller Connell, K. Y., Armstrong, C. M., & Musgrove, S. L. (2013). Assessing sustainability education in a transdisciplinary undergraduate course focused on real-world problem solving: A case for disciplinary grounding. *International Journal of Sustainability in Higher Education, 14*(4), 404–433.

Rhodes, J., Reddy, R., Roffman, J., & Grossman, J. B. (2005). Promoting successful youth mentoring relationships: A preliminary screening questionnaire. *Journal of Primary Prevention, 26*, 147–167.

Rhodes, J. E., Spencer, R., Keller, T. E., Liang, B., & Noam, G. (2006). A model for the influence of mentoring relationships on youth development. *Journal of Community Psychology, 34*(6), 691–707.

Ritz, J. M., & Fan, S.-C. (2015). STEM and technology education: International state-of-the-art. *International Journal of Technology and Design Education, 25*, 429–451.

Roberts, L. F., & Wassersug, R. J. (2009). Does doing scientific research in high school correlate with students staying in science? A half-century retrospective study. *Research in Science Education, 39*, 251–256.

Robnett, R. D., Chemers, M. M., & Zurbriggen, E. L. (2015). Longitudinal associations among undergraduates' research experience, self-efficacy, and identity. *Journal of Research in Science Teaching, 52*(6), 847–867.

References

Rogers, M., Pfaff, T., Hamilton, J., & Erkan, A. (2015). Using sustainability themes and multidisciplinary approaches to enhance STEM education. *International Journal of Sustainability in Higher Education, 16*(4), 523–536.

Roth, W. M., & Roychoudhury, A. (1993). The development of science process skills in authentic contexts. *Journal of Research in Science Teaching, 30*(2), 127–152.

Sabirova, E. G., & Zakirova, V. G. (2015). Formation of pupils' research skills in informational and educational environment of elementary school. *Procedia-Social and Behavioral Sciences, 191*, 1139–1142.

Sadler, T. D., Burgin, S., McKinney, L., & Ponjuan, L. (2010). Learning science through research apprenticeships: A critical review of the literature. *Journal of Research in Science Teaching: THe Official Journal of the National Association for Research in Science Teaching, 47*(3), 235–256. https://doi.org/10.1002/tea.20326

Sasson, I. (2019). Participation in research apprenticeship program: Issues related to career choice in STEM. *International Journal of Science and Mathematics Education, 17*, 467–482.

Schwartz, R. S., & Crawford, B. A. (2006). Authentic scientific inquiry as context for teaching nature of science: Identifying critical element. In *Scientific inquiry and nature of science: Implications for teaching, learning, and teacher education* (pp. 331–355). Springer.

Schwartzman, R. (2013). Reviving a digital dinosaur: Text-only synchronous online chats and peer tutoring in communication centers. *College Student Journal, 47*(4), 653–667.

Shang, H. (2021, March). Connecting chemistry to mathematics by establishing the relationship between conductivity and concentration in an interdisciplinary, computer-based project for high school chemistry students. *Journal of Chemical Education, 98*(3), 796–804. https://doi.org/10.1021/acs.jchemed.0c01179

Sharpe, R., Abrahams, I., & Fotou, N. (2018). Does paired mentoring work? A study of the effectiveness and affective value of academically asymmetrical peer mentoring in supporting disadvantaged students in school science. *Research in Science & Technological Education, 36*(2), 205–225.

Swan, A. K., Inkelas, K. K., Jones, J. N., & Pretlow, J. The Role of High School Research Experiences in the Development of Undergraduate Students' Research Self-Efficacy.

Swan, A. K., Inkelas, K. K., Jones, J. N., Pretlow, J., & Keller, T. F. (2018). The role of high school research experiences in shaping students' research self-efficacy and preparation for undergraduate research participation. *Journal of the First-Year Experience & Students in Transition, 30*(1), 103–120.

Tai, R. H., Kong, X., Mitchell, C. E., Dabney, K. P., Read, D. M., Jeffe, D. B., Andriole, D. A., & Wathington, H. D. (2017). Examining summer laboratory research apprenticeships for high school students as a factor in entry to MD/PhD programs at matriculation. *CBE—Life Sciences Education, 16*(2), ar37. https://doi.org/10.1187/cbe.15-07-0161

Tai, R. H., Qi Liu, C., Maltese, A. V., & Fan, X. (2006). Planning early for careers in science. *Science, 312*(5777), 1143–1144. https://doi.org/10.1126/science.1128690

Ten Cate, O., & Durning, S. (2007). Dimensions and psychology of peer teaching in medical education. *Medical Teacher, 29*(6), 546–552.

Ten Cate, O., van de Vorst, I., & van den Broek, S. (2012). Academic achievement of students tutored by near-peers. *International Journal of Medical Education, 3*.

Thiry, H., & Laursen, S. L. (2011). The role of student-advisor interactions in apprenticing undergraduate researchers into a scientific community of practice. *Journal of Science Education and Technology, 20*, 771–784.

Ward, E. G., Thomas, E. E., & Disch, W. B. (2014). Mentor service themes emergent in a holistic, undergraduate peer-mentoring experience. *Journal of College Student Development, 55*(6), 563–579.

Woods, D. R., Hrymak, A. N., Marshall, R. R., Wood, P. E., Crowe, C. M., Hoffman, T. W., Wright, J. D., Taylor, P. A., Woodhouse, K. A., & Bouchard, C. K. (1997). Developing problem solving skills: The McMaster problem solving program. *Journal of Engineering Education, 86*(2), 75–91.

Open Access This chapter is licensed under the terms of the Creative Commons Attribution 4.0 International License (http://creativecommons.org/licenses/by/4.0/), which permits use, sharing, adaptation, distribution and reproduction in any medium or format, as long as you give appropriate credit to the original author(s) and the source, provide a link to the Creative Commons license and indicate if changes were made.

The images or other third party material in this chapter are included in the chapter's Creative Commons license, unless indicated otherwise in a credit line to the material. If material is not included in the chapter's Creative Commons license and your intended use is not permitted by statutory regulation or exceeds the permitted use, you will need to obtain permission directly from the copyright holder.

Chapter 5
Transforming Undergraduate Research Experiences Through RCT

Abstract Chapter 5, titled "RCT in Undergraduate Research Experience Environment," examines the evolution and impact of undergraduate research experiences (UREs) in fostering research-driven cognitive behaviors. Once primarily the domain of graduate studies, research experiences are increasingly incorporated into undergraduate education, providing students with valuable opportunities to enhance critical thinking, problem-solving, and employability skills.

The chapter explores the contribution of UREs, including course-based undergraduate research experiences (CUREs), to the development of essential cognitive skills such as analytical thinking, teamwork, and lifelong learning. It highlights the role of research-based learning (RBL) in shaping student behavior and the importance of a dynamic learning environment in nurturing these skills.

Drawing on a range of studies, the chapter emphasizes the benefits of early exposure to research activities and the significant influence of faculty mentorship in developing research self-efficacy and professional growth. It also addresses the challenges faced by faculty in engaging students in research and the strategies employed to overcome these challenges.

Additionally, the chapter provides a detailed analysis of the CURE model, including its adaptation in university settings and its effectiveness in enhancing work readiness and scientific thinking. Through case studies and empirical evidence, it illustrates how CUREs contribute to cognitive, psychosocial, and behavioral outcomes, aligning with Research Cognitive Theory (RCT). The chapter concludes by discussing the application of CUREs in research internship programs, emphasizing their role in preparing undergraduate students for the demands of the modern workforce.

5.1 Research Cognitive Behavior Development in an Undergraduate Research Environment

Earlier, Research experiences were restricted to learners pursuing a Master's or Ph.D., totally unrelated to student coursework and assignments, and hence, no research-driven behavior development, both cognitive and intellectual was expected or targeted. However, with the introduction of UREs, the significance of fostering research behavior started grabbing attention as it has been linked to developing the skills associated with critical thinking, problem-solving, and employability skills, especially in research-based workplaces that employ graduates (Bandaranaike & Willison, 2015; Missingham et al., 2018; Wass et al., 2011; Willison et al., 2017; Wilmore & Willison, 2016). UREs were closely associated with explicit research skill development that readily enhances learners' behavior especially generic skills that include investigation, analytical thinking, teamwork, communication, lifelong learning, and emotional and cultural awareness. Research-driven cognitive behavior development is normally enacted through diverse Research-Based Learning (RBL), integrated activities embedded in course curriculum as well as in informal co-curricular mentored research like UREs or research internship programs. RBL, often synonymously used as inquiry-based learning in most of the research studies has offered us a robust literature background on the conceptual understanding of different cognitive skills associated with UG learners. Though these studies offer insight into the developed research skills and behavior, they also advocate the role of a dynamic environment that has contributed to the maturity of these skills. For example, a recent large-scale multidisciplinary study conducted on UG students from Australia discovered that graduates who displayed their 'generic' skills were polished during their UG years in a research-based environment. This study also vouched for the increasing research productivity in a research-based working environment, when the learners were exposed to early research activities (Gelso, 1973, 1993; Gelso et al., 1996; Hollingsworth & Fassinger, 2002; Kahn & Scott, 1997; KREBS, 1991).

Similarly, earlier research has revealed that many informal programs approved by the American Psychological Association (APA) have instilled early hands-on experiences in clinical areas, while similar activities were less common in research (Galassi et al., 1986). This study also emphasized the significant role of faculty members in contributing to the students' development as researchers. The study cited that faculty members during research-based training, are vital to modeling learner behavior and attitudes, which exactly aligns to the RCT, that focuses on the role of social interactions in developing positive cognitive behavior in research. As the research faculty display enthusiasm about research, in its underlying theories and innovative ideas, eventually nurturing learners' interest in research. The study also pinpoints the stand taken by research faculty in addressing the limitations that they encounter while performing research and normalizing the challenges that UG learners may face. In fact, this study was executed on the framework of theory of research training environment (RTE) by Gelso (1993). Gelso in his study also discusses on the role of faculty in building a research training environment that can contribute to the development of graduate learner's research attitudes and research productivity.

Also, the role of faculty in making interventions in the social aspects of research is important. The capacity of research mentors to address the social and interpersonal needs of learners by guaranteeing mentor–mentee relationship and research community collaborations is crucial. This was observed by earlier research conducted by Krebs and colleagues who discovered that research productivity was witnessed higher for the learners who engaged in research as a social experience (KREBS, 1991).

In general, studies reported on enhancing UG learners' research self-efficacy as they are exposed to a positive research training environment that expose students to early research experience as in UREs, in the presence of an active social environment that include research faculty (Hollingsworth & Fassinger, 2002; Phillips & Russell, 1994). For example, Psychology based programs present dynamic environment with research experiences that involve learners mainly in collaborative tasks, dissemination of research findings thereby ensuring active communication and executing individual research projects, as in dissertation or thesis completion. Love and research team also conducted an experimental study to discover the influences that determine the research self-efficacy and discovered that similar factors like thesis presentation and collaborative team work had an impact on research self-efficacy (Love et al., 2007). The mixed method study was successful in addressing graduate learners about their research experiences in terms of quality to determine the attributes associated with the research efficacy and productivity.

Studies related to establishing the individual perceptions of students based on their experience were also equally important in establishing RCT along with the studies that offered insights into the research learning environment. As such, we hereafter discuss the perceived learning outcomes of UREs. Bauer and Bennett (2003) report in their study about development of 'general cognitive and personal abilities and skills' and the correlation between them with subject to the UG research (Bauer & Bennett, 2003). The study exhibited the development of eight identified cognitive skills and aspiration to pursue higher degrees in study participants in comparison to the non-participants. Similarly, research performed by Ward and colleagues (2002) indicated that research participants perceived enhanced learning behavior in the research context, i.e. intellectual learning in comparison to the lecture based courses (Ward et al., 2002). Participants in their study along with that of the study performed by Reisberg (1998) also perceived satisfaction in developing technical skills, i.e.. Cognitive behavior as they expressed their intrinsic motivation while performing research (Reisberg, 1998). Cognitive behavior development was exhibited by the student researchers in the form of skills and attitudes that include both professional and individual growth, career aspirations and scientific thinking (Seymour et al., 2004). Some studies also forthright present their evidences on the motivation provided by the students to the research faculty to further their progress in their research, which in fact supports the RCT where a reciprocity of the social environment and cognitive behavior of individuals is validly stated (Evans & Witkosky, 2004; Jonte-Pace, 2003).

Despite of the positive interpretation on the co-habitation of research environment and research cognitive behavior, there were concerns on the different challenges encountered by faculty in engaging student researchers (Evans & Witkosky, 2004; Reisberg, 1998) (Healey, 2005). However, in accordance with the principle of Dewey, that defines learning as a result of discovery paved under mentoring rather than transmission of information (p. 15), it is preferred to encourage UG learners to associate with different research based programs like UREs and research internship programs (Dewey, 1997). These programs have reputedly proved to be as highly efficient as in any skill development programs by executing highly intellectual learning processes in a extensively collaborative environment that promote enhanced scientific thinking, problem solving and communication. On the grounds of the revolutionary findings from the above studies, UG learners were introduced to UREs that engaged UG learners in the research environment under the mentorship of research faculty. In the later sections, we will be reeling into UREs and their evolution into CUREs, in addition to research internship programs thereby presenting different perspectives on the existence of RCT under different research settings.

5.2 Course-based Undergraduate Research Experiences (CURE) Model and Adaptation of RCT to Enhance Work Readiness

Undergraduate Research experiences (URE) are widely practiced across most universities to foster research attitudes, aspirations, and diverse work skills. As we discuss the work skills specifically in a research environment, the normally practiced methods include employing undergraduate (UG) in faculty research, and evolving outcomes such as critical thinking and efficacy (Kilgo et al., 2015; Kuh, 2008). UREs persuade UG learners to acquire knowledge in the research process, perform literature reviews, and be involved in the analytical and interpretation of data. In the process, learners adapt to different challenges and subsequently develop tolerance to barriers, thereby evolving into independent research learners (Lopatto, 2003). Learners enhance their ability to think, get curious, and be inspired, prompting them to solve problems and become adept in the UG courses or disciplines that they are pursuing (McCune & Hounsell, 2005). As they gain confidence in subject-based knowledge, they are more likely to persist in their UG programs with career transparency and better self-efficacy. Learners pursuing science-related careers are able to retain their research interest and thereby transfer their positive subject-based outlook in exhibiting retention in their UG programs (Russell et al., 2007a). Chemistry classrooms in universities define UREs as a high-impact practice for advocating equity and success, thereby contributing to mentoring students for workforce training, wherein these two skills hold a major value. UREs have managed to grab the attention of employers with their contribution to developing work skills like resilience, communication, critical thinking, and collaboration skills. Though there is no argument on the effect of UREs on the development of professional skills and learning outcome attainment in UG students, it is necessary to not overlook one of its major limitations that it cannot engage a large pool of learners within a limited research setting. Course-based undergraduate research experiences (CUREs) were introduced to the university premises to solve this flaw, thereby involving a considerably higher number of undergraduates in science course-based research. Diverse studies conducted on the effectiveness of the CURE model have reported to offer the same outcomes as that of traditional UREs. The different stages of CURE model implementation as discussed in Chapter 1, can offer sufficient prospectives for the UG students to develop different skills crucial for the workforce (Jordan et al., 2014; Rowland et al., 2012; Shaffer et al., 2014). Studies of CUREs have offered similar reports to that conducted on UREs, demonstrating student gains in research attitudes, and research skills, especially self-efficacy, and college persistence in science majors (Harrison et al., 2011; Jordan et al., 2014; Lopatto, 2003; Lopatto et al., 2008; Rowland et al., 2012; Shaffer et al., 2014). A CURE-based curriculum enables students to approach unique, feasible, and applicable research questions, thereby training them in faculty research and ensuring student learning (Ballen et al., 2017). CURE-based courses have been reported to enhance learners' interest, favor laboratory experiences, thereby transforming them into a "Think like a scientist" mode (Brownell et al., 2012a).

Many universities have introduced CUREs to their classrooms and laboratories to engage several UG learners in research at one time, or to accommodate all students enrolled in a particular course (Auchincloss et al., 2014). CURE model was initially applied in biology-based courses at the university, exploring different knowledge gains at different college levels, as reported by different studies. The study by Brownell and his colleagues offered more insight into the effect of CURE based course (Brownell et al., 2012a). CURE model was incorporated into randomly allocated laboratory segments of a sizable introductory biology course at a public university. The model offered a more favorable experience than conventional labs and yielded specific improvements in knowledge acquisition, as the study was based on a follow-up assessment of the learners as they progressed through the biology course. The study employed surveys on knowledge assessments and learner perceptions at the adjourning of their mandatory courses, as required in the biology major. The research study weighed whether the provisional gains of the introductory-level CURE on learner knowledge and perception are continual throughout their college years from sophomore to final year. Learners who participated in the CURE based course when compared to control perceived a greater understanding of what researchers perform and a boosted interest in pursuing a research career. The study finally concluded that targeted knowledge gains persisted throughout their college years from sophomore to final, meanwhile prediction models pointed on the necessity of carrying out multiple CUREs to sustain perception gains throughout a learner's college years. This research as targeting the perceptions that define the behavior of the students apart from their intellectual knowledge provides a perfect example on the adaptation of RCT, as CURE model provides a suitable dynamic learning environment for the behavior development. A similar study by Brownell and his team, conducted on a

CURE-based course, targets introductory biology students to learn about the characterization of single point mutations in p53, a tumor suppressor gene that is mutated in more than 50% of human cancers. The data collection instruments included open-ended written prompts, which offered insight into the change in student perspectives on what it means to think like a scientist as a rookie to be more professional. This study clearly focused on building learner behavior under a CURE based research setting. Learners successfully acknowledged experimental repetition, data analysis, and collaboration as significant aspects of thinking like a scientist at the end of the course. Assessments on the course also revealed that learners revealed growth in their analytical and interpretation abilities. The study provided a solid conclusion on the positive impact of CURE-based course on the development of students' conceptions and practice of scientific thinking (Brownell et al., 2015).

Another study was based on a course called Soakin' Up the Rays (SUR) with S. that integrated all five CURE steps (Wolkow et al., 2019). Initially, learners conducted a yeast genetic screen as it placed the learners in a dynamic environment that could grab their attention to make discoveries in search of potentially novel mutations that influence DNA damage responses. Consequently, the learners performed inquiry-related research steps to develop an understanding of the research objectives. Learners then engaged in collaborative tasks with their peers thereby building a research rapport as they collected data, generated graphs, and interpreted raw data to characterize the mutants they produced. Next, learners unleashed their abilities by carrying out diverse scientific practices such as modeling, statistical, computational, and visualization techniques thereby building new scientific knowledge and expertise. Finally, learners developed tangible outcomes that involved replica plating, phenotypic analyses and multiple serial dilutions that reinforced their iterative knowledge and skills. In the due process, the CURE setting has based the dynamic research environment where the learners developed intellectually both in their extrinsic knowledge as well as their (Wolkow et al., 2019).

Most of the literature reviews that offers insight into the effectiveness of CURE model adaptation is focused on lower-level courses at university (Brownell et al., 2012b; Govindan et al., 2020). However, recently, upper-level courses that tend to be more focused and of a smaller population with experienced learners are also adapting CURE models to practice research-based activities (Beatty et al., 2021). While understanding the underlying theories that scaffold the CURE model, it is crucial to manifest how its implementation affects the outcomes of the learners. CUREs are widely explained as "scalable laboratory learning environments" for subjecting students to early research, which becomes challenging in upper-level courses due to the course complexity. In this case, instructors have a major role in defining the learning environment, as they offer structured learning content prior to motivating the students to practice research independently. This case was observed in a study by (Beatty et al., 2021), where the instructors/ faculty mentors offer training to the learners to develop methodological skills quintessential to successfully complete distinct research projects. This practice also aligns with the RCT, as a dynamic research environment is constructed through this structured course format, with the aim of encouraging learner curiosity, autonomy, and creativity within the CURE framework. In the study, major skill building is focused on preparing the learners to employ research skills to address diverse scientific challenges. The limitation of such a structured format is that the process may follow a linear stride to a desired outcome with controlled autonomy witnessing a particular behavior. Hence, a balance between learner autonomy and desired behavior, the two learning environment constituents must be considered by the faculty while developing the dynamic structured research environment with adequate room for research skill development or learner independence that drives their creative imagination and innovation in solving problems. Also the faculty should not overlook the learner needs thereby witnessing an inverse relationship between the two learning environment constituents. As the faculty engages in developing the CURE based course formats, social interactions between the learner individual, environment and behavior come into play. When a learner individual is considered, his/her skill sets need to be considered by the faculty to set appropriate research skill building as CURE courses often accommodate diverse learner groups with both soft and advanced skill sets. Faculty needs to be cognizant in designing lesson experiences, i.e. research environment, that offer a balance between offering learner autonomy as well as assisting them in retaining already existing skills. While considering the learner behavior, faculty needs to set protocols that are not more complex and demand advanced skill set, to not off the learner confidence levels, which may negatively influence the research skill development goals. Learners also need to be informed of the professional applicability of the skills, so that they may strive more to develop their abilities in completing a research task and relate it to its relevance to their future career pathways (Wieman, 2017).These studies have adopted SLT as their theoretical foundation, however, by exploring both cognitive and social elements, reliant on mental processing and construction, it is clearly aligned to the RCT. The studies elaborate on the relationship of the social context wherein the learners observe and interact with the research community that include peers and research faculty. CUREs are developed in line with the concepts of situated learning as learners perform the tasks that scientists do (e.g., inquire, design methods, collect and analyze data, frame conclusive models) by tackling real scientific situations. However, as most of the desired outcomes of CURE adaptation that include cognitive behavior and intellectual learning is being discussed in majority of the studies, we believe, RCT is suitably the most closely associated theory that could hold the CURE model. This could be more elaborately understood as we explain the different CURE based approaches that have been adopted in different university level courses.

According to the RCT, all the studies discussed above provided the students with an environment that guaranteed active learning by engaging the learners with hands on experience, developing their skills in performing scientific research. The environment also involved them in social rapport especially with peer collaboration thereby polishing their communication skills apart from the 21st century skills. These studies have proved that engaged learners accomplish the same outcomes as those who complete research experiences in typical UREs. We have come to the conclusion that CUREs are highly impactful in involving UG students to participate in a novel array of activities resulting in gradual accomplishment of different cognitive, psychosocial, and behavioral outcomes. However, CUREs vary extensively in their design and execution, and there is lesser clarity to the aspects of CUREs that are vital and adequate to accomplish desired learner outcomes. Multiple studies have highlighted on the learner outcomes associated with UG learners who perform CUREs in research internship environment (Jordan et al., 2014; Rowland et al., 2012; Shaffer et al., 2014). We have also adopted CURE model in a research internship wherein we can detail the adaptation of RCT in research internship environments and the development of learner outcomes.

5.3 RCT in CURE Based Research Internship Programs

When it comes to the workplace, employers are looking forward to accommodating skilled employees to ensure enhanced productivity and sustainability. As such, it is important to develop skills in the ready to graduate UG students especially with workplace skills. There exists a myriad of skills that are highly relevant to each work responsibility. For instance, some employees need to be technically superior, as in the case of equipment handlers, on the other hand, others need to be analytically higher in thinking, as in the case of analysts, scientists and researchers (Hull et al., 1982). Meanwhile, another dimension demands employees to exhibit distinct qualities such as punctuality, dependability, and persistence (Bowles & Gintis, 2000; Dreeben, 1968) to ensure success at their workplace, being nurtured at an early age in from school or similar social environment. Based on the study performed by Kohn, in 1986 positive associations among problem-solving skill, educational attainment, and occupational status, was discovered (Kohn, 1987). As such, an invisible tension was experienced by the educational community to design diverse educational activities both curricular and non-curricular across all learner stages according to the demands of the employers and job market. This gave inception to the concept of Outcomes-based education (OBE) which was later extensively used in the 1980's to accomplish predetermined target learning outcomes. OBE promoted the development of a structured learning environment, which formed the basis for creating an outcomes-driven research internship program for undergraduate students (Spady, 1988). Before commencing the discussion on the rationale behind adopting OBE into research internship program (RIP), it is important to understand the normally practiced approaches and learning outcomes with UG RIPs.

RIPs are time-restricted educational programs that engage learners in performing research-based activities in a research setting at a research center/ educational institution. Traditional RIPs often engage UG students in collaborative research tasks under the mentorship of a research faculty mentor using a stand-alone approach (Galeano et al., 2012). During the internship that takes place in a duration of a couple of weeks to months, participants develop different research skills and enhance their attitudes as similar to UREs. Though UREs integrate limited number of student researchers into collaborative research groups, RIPs conventionally extend a classroom experience beyond classrooms, by enabling learners to address the gaps in the contextual classroom to outlive the workplace challenges (Callanan & Benzing, 2004). As

5.3 RCT in CURE Based Research Internship Programs

such RIP participants sharpen their skills, enhance their knowledge, and broaden their perspectives to pave a smooth transition to the workplace from their college years (Kapareliotis et al., 2019). The distinct feature of RIPs that contrasts with the functionality of a URE is that RIPs are not necessarily outcome-based and usually culminate without a distinct tangible outcome. Conventional RIPs normally require participants to submit reports that state their experience during the confined time limits, which indeed do not offer students with measurable recognition other than a participation certificate. Meanwhile, RIPs focus on cognitive behavior development, thereby motivating students to divert or pave their future depending on the positive perceptions gained by the participants during the program (Council, 2003; Lopatto, 2003). The pros of similar interventions have been documented anecdotally as well as empirically spanning across diverse institutions and implementation methods (Linn et al., 2015; Lopatto, 2003; National Academies of Sciences, 2017; Russell et al., 2007b).

As it is imperative to measure the efficiency of learning interventions to document the student learning behavior, traditional RIPs do not offer support with lack of valid assessment strategies or evaluation and monitoring. As such, most of the RIPs are not well documented as scholarly work, thereby widening the gaps in literature. To curb this, we recently developed a novel CURE based RIP (see Figure 5.1) that culminated with tangible outcomes. We executed an outcomes driven RIP that clearly aimed at developing specific sill sets in addition to tangible outcomes such as scholarly publication or working prototype. CUREs have evidently proven to be effective in developing research cognitive behavior in learners as discussed in the previous section along the participants from different disciplines and across different college years. Our model, a novel and distinctive approach successfully engages students in a dynamic research environment, wherein they interact with the research community, as they progress through the CURE based research steps, getting excited to accomplish their research goals within a specific time frame of 2–4 weeks. However, once the students are intrinsically motivated, they continue their research and work collaboratively to present scientific publications in conferences and journals. This model frames a dynamic research environment, catering to establish the guidelines set forward for the research faculty thereby ensuring high quality to the research projects and their execution. The model encourages faculty to adopt and practice multi-disciplinary research as integrated STEM so as to inform and educate the students of the benefits of performing a multidisciplinary research. This model was built as a conclusive interpretation and was drawn out on the mixed methods carried out to evaluate the effectiveness of the model by comparing the performance of both participants and non—participants. The participants of the outcomes-based RIPs were initially offered a research methodology course followed by active research activities. As the students undertake course sessions on how to perform a literature review, on the following day, the participant engages in PRISMA to perform a literature review. Similarly, a concurrent system is being followed to carry out the research activities thereby ensuring immediate transfer of knowledge resulting in the applicability of the acquired knowledge. The model as shown below ensures that the participant culminates with a distinct outcome that is measurable.

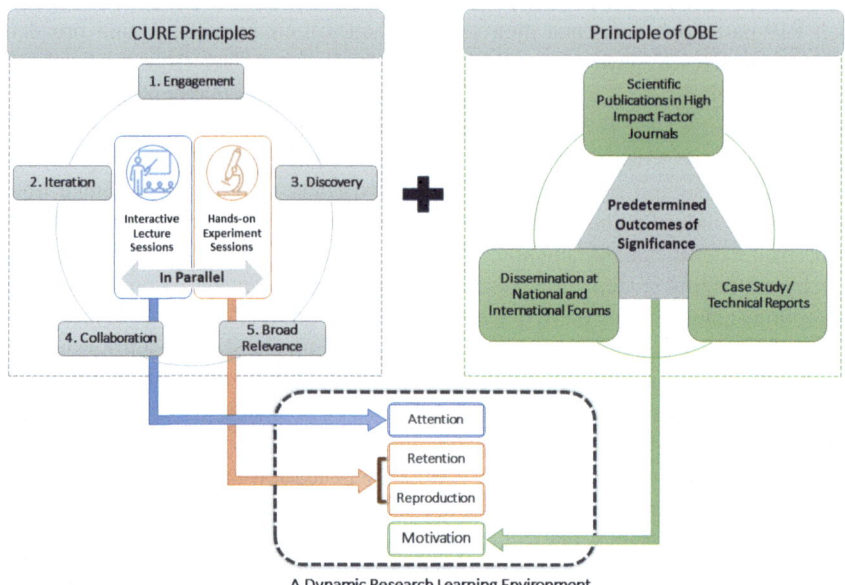

Fig. 5.1 Outcomes-Driven Research Internship Program (RIP). This figure illustrates the structured methodology of the Outcomes-Driven RIP model, emphasizing concurrent knowledge transfer, multidisciplinary collaboration, and tangible results such as publications or prototypes. It highlights the program's dynamic research environment designed to enhance participants' research competencies, technical skills, and teamwork capabilities within a defined timeframe. Reproduced with permission from (Siby et al., 2024) (Copyright Emerald Publishing Limited, 2024)

The data analysis of the participant performance exhibited enhanced students' research competency confidence in comparison to the non-participants. This indeed is in line with the studies conducted on CURE models (National Academies of Sciences, 2017) by reinforcing the students' acquired knowledge through experiential learning in enhancing the cognitive behavior. The model proved effective in increasing the student perceptions on performing research, exhibiting technical skills, teamwork, preparing scientific poster/ write a research article and writing a technical report. As this model adopted a multidisciplinary research environment to create a dynamic learning environment suitable for intellectual learning, the model also ensured that social interactions are active within the research community that accommodates researchers from multidisciplinary background. For example, in the project titled, "Artificial Intelligence for Detection of Dental Pathology", the researchers hail from computer engineering and dental medicine thereby training students from both the backgrounds. As such, the individual exposed to similar environment develop to adapt and persevere in the adversity of challenges that encounter them. This is a classical representation of establishing RCT, which advocates on the reciprocity of the social interactions that takes place in an active learning environment.

5.4 Chapter Summary

In this chapter, the focus shifts to transforming undergraduate research experiences (UREs) through the lens of Research Cognitive Theory (RCT). Historically, research opportunities were confined to advanced academic levels and rarely aligned with undergraduate coursework, leaving cognitive and research behavior development untapped. However, the advent of UREs marked a paradigm shift, emphasizing critical thinking, problem-solving, and employability skills within research-driven environments. Studies reveal that integrating research into undergraduate education fosters intellectual growth, nurtures scientific thinking, and enhances personal and professional skills. Faculty mentors play a pivotal role, modeling enthusiasm, addressing challenges, and fostering a supportive research culture that aligns with RCT principles, which emphasize the interplay between social contexts and cognitive behavior.

The chapter delves into the Course-Based Undergraduate Research Experience (CURE) model, a scalable solution to traditional URE limitations. By integrating research into course curricula, CUREs engage larger student groups, offering experiences that mirror real-world scientific inquiry. These courses emphasize collaboration, critical analysis, and hands-on learning, fostering both cognitive and social development. Research illustrates that CUREs not only bolster research self-efficacy and persistence in STEM disciplines but also instill a "think like a scientist" mindset. From introductory to advanced levels, these models adapt to diverse educational contexts, creating dynamic environments that stimulate curiosity, autonomy, and innovation. CURE-based approaches embody the principles of RCT, wherein students actively engage in research processes, collaborate with peers, and align their academic pursuits with professional aspirations.

The chapter concludes with an exploration of CURE-based research internship programs, which bridge academic learning with workplace readiness. These programs emphasize outcome-driven education, culminating in tangible achievements such as publications or prototypes. By fostering multidisciplinary collaborations and integrating real-world applications, these internships create robust learning environments that enhance students' research competencies and teamwork skills. Such initiatives demonstrate the reciprocity central to RCT, where dynamic social interactions within research communities enrich cognitive behavior and intellectual growth. The chapter highlights the transformative potential of embedding RCT principles into undergraduate research, empowering students to navigate academic and professional challenges with confidence and adaptability.

Glossary

Undergraduate Research Experience (URE) Research opportunities integrated into undergraduate education, focusing on fostering critical thinking, problem-solving, and research skills

Course-Based Undergraduate Research Experience (CURE) A scalable model that incorporates research into course curricula, enabling larger student groups to engage in scientific inquiry

Research Cognitive Theory (RCT) A theoretical framework that highlights the interaction between social contexts and cognitive behavior in research environments

Research Training Environment (RTE) A framework emphasizing the role of faculty and research culture in developing students' research attitudes and productivity

Generic Skills Broad competencies such as critical thinking, teamwork, communication, and analytical reasoning applicable across disciplines

Research Self-Efficacy Confidence in one's ability to conduct research effectively, often developed through hands-on experiences and mentorship

Dynamic Learning Environment An interactive and supportive setting that fosters active learning, collaboration, and innovation among students

Think Like a Scientist A mindset emphasizing scientific thinking, inquiry, experimentation, and evidence-based reasoning

Social Learning Theory (SLT) A theory emphasizing learning through observation, imitation, and interaction with others

Outcomes-Based Education (OBE) An educational framework focusing on achieving specific learning outcomes through structured and measurable interventions

Research Internship Program (RIP) Time-limited educational programs where students engage in research-based activities under mentorship, often culminating in tangible outcomes

Multidisciplinary Research Research that integrates knowledge and methodologies from multiple disciplines to address complex problems

21st-Century Skills Competencies like critical thinking, collaboration, communication, and adaptability essential for modern workplaces

Research Productivity The output of research activities, including publications, prototypes, or scientific advancements, reflecting research engagement

Active Learning An instructional approach that involves hands-on, participatory activities to engage students in the learning process

Intrinsic Motivation Internal drive to engage in activities for personal satisfaction and intellectual growth rather than external rewards

Faculty Mentorship Guidance provided by faculty members to support students' research skills, attitudes, and professional development

Situated Learning A concept where learning occurs in a real-world context, closely mirroring the practices of professionals in the field

Dynamic Research Environment A setting that combines hands-on experimentation, collaboration, and mentorship to foster active learning and critical skills

Outcome-Driven Research Internship Program A research internship model focused on achieving specific, measurable outcomes such as publications or prototypes

Cognitive Behavior Development The process of enhancing skills and attitudes such as critical thinking, problem-solving, and scientific reasoning

Reciprocity in Research The mutual interaction between learners and their research environment, fostering both cognitive and social growth

Collaborative Learning An approach where students work together to solve problems, complete tasks, or create projects, enhancing teamwork skills

References

Auchincloss, L. C., Laursen, S. L., Branchaw, J. L., Eagan, K., Graham, M., Hanauer, D. I., Lawrie, G., McLinn, C. M., Pelaez, N., & Rowland, S. (2014). Assessment of course-based undergraduate research experiences: a meeting report. *CBE—Life Sciences Education, 13*(1), 29–40.

Ballen, C. J., Wieman, C., Salehi, S., Searle, J. B., & Zamudio, K. R. (2017). Enhancing diversity in undergraduate science: Self-efficacy drives performance gains with active learning. *CBE—Life Sciences Education, 16*(4), ar56.

Bandaranaike, S., & Willison, J. (2015). *Building capacity for work-readiness: Bridging the cognitive and affective domains.*

Bauer, K. W., & Bennett, J. S. (2003). Alumni perceptions used to assess undergraduate research experience. *The Journal of Higher Education, 74*(2), 210–230.

Beatty, A. E., Ballen, C. J., Driessen, E. P., Schwartz, T. S., & Graze, R. M. (2021). Addressing the unique qualities of upper-level biology course-based undergraduate research experiences through the integration of skill-building. *Integrative and Comparative Biology, 61*(3), 981–991. https://doi.org/10.1093/icb/icab006

Bowles, S., & Gintis, H. (2000). Reciprocity, self-interest, and the welfare state. *Nordic Journal of Political Economy, 26*(1), 33–53.

Brownell, S. E., Hekmat-Scafe, D. S., Singla, V., Seawell, P. C., Imam, J. F. C., Eddy, S. L., Stearns, T., & Cyert, M. S. (2015). A high-enrollment course-based undergraduate research experience improves student conceptions of scientific thinking and ability to interpret data. *CBE—Life Sciences Education, 14*(2), ar21. https://doi.org/10.1187/cbe.14-05-0092

Brownell, S. E., Kloser, M. J., Fukami, T., & Shavelson, R. (2012a). Undergraduate biology lab courses: Comparing the impact of traditionally based "cookbook" and authentic research-based courses on student lab experiences. *Journal of College Science Teaching, 41*(4), 36–45.

Brownell, S. E., Kloser, M. J., Fukami, T., & Shavelson, R. (2012b). Undergraduate biology lab courses: Comparing the impact of traditionally based" cookbook" and authentic research-based courses on student lab experiences. *Journal of College Science Teaching, 41*(4).

Callanan, G., & Benzing, C. (2004). Assessing the role of internships in the career-oriented employment of graduating college students. *Education+ training, 46*(2), 82–89.

Council, N. R. (2003). *BIO2010: Transforming undergraduate education for future research biologists.*

Dewey, J. (1997). Experience and education. *The Educational Forum, 1938–8098, 50*(3), 241–252. . https://www.concrete.org/students/studentcompetitions/frcbowlingballcompetition.aspx#:~:text=The%20objective%20of%20this%20competition,in%20engineering%20design%20and%20analysis.

Dreeben, R. (1968). On what is learned in school.

Evans, R., & Witkosky, D. (2004). Who gives a damn what they think anyway?: Involving students in mentored research. *National Social Science Journal, 23*(1), 21–30.

Galassi, J. P., Brooks, L., Stoltz, R. F., & Trexler, K. A. (1986). Research training environments and student productivity: An exploratory study. *The Counseling Psychologist, 14*(1), 31–36.

Galeano, N., Morales-Menendez, R., & Cantú, F. J. (2012). Developing research skills in undergraduate students through an internship program in research and innovation. *International Journal of Engineering Education, 28*(1), 48.

Gelso, C. J. (1973). Effect of audiorecording and videorecording on client satisfaction and self-expression. *Journal of Consulting and Clinical Psychology, 40*(3), 455.

Gelso, C. J. (1993). On the making of a scientist-practitioner: A theory of research training in professional psychology. *Professional Psychology: Research and Practice, 24*(4), 468–476. https://doi.org/10.1037/0735-7028.24.4.468

Gelso, C. J., Mallinckrodt, B., & Judge, A. B. (1996). Research training environment, attitudes toward research, and research self-efficacy: The revised Research Training Environment Scale. *The Counseling Psychologist, 24*(2), 304–322.

Govindan, B., Pickett, S., & Riggs, B. (2020). Fear of the CURE: A beginner's guide to overcoming barriers in creating a course-based undergraduate research experience. *Journal of Microbiology & Biology Education, 21*(2), 50.

Harrison, M., Dunbar, D., Ratmansky, L., Boyd, K., & Lopatto, D. (2011). Classroom-based science research at the introductory level: changes in career choices and attitude. *CBE—Life Sciences Education, 10*(3), 279–286.

Healey, M. (2005). Linking research and teaching to benefit student learning. *Journal of Geography in Higher Education, 29*(2), 183–201.

Hollingsworth, M. A., & Fassinger, R. E. (2002). The role of faculty mentors in the research training of counseling psychology doctoral students. *Journal of Counseling Psychology, 49*(3), 324.

Hull, F. M., Friedman, N. S., & Rogers, T. F. (1982). The effect of technology on alienation from work: Testing Blauner's inverted U-curve hypothesis for 110 industrial organizations and 245 retrained printers. *Work and Occupations, 9*(1), 31–57.

Jonte-Pace, D. (2003). Enhancing the research-teaching nexus. *The Teaching Scholar: The Newsletter of the Faculty Development Program, Santa Clara University, 2*(1).

Jordan, T. C., Burnett, S. H., Carson, S., Caruso, S. M., Clase, K., DeJong, R. J., Dennehy, J. J., Denver, D. R., Dunbar, D., & Elgin, S. C. (2014). A broadly implementable research course in phage discovery and genomics for first-year undergraduate students. *MBio, 5*(1), https://doi.org/10.1128/mbio.01051-01013

Kahn, J. H., & Scott, N. A. (1997). Predictors of research productivity and science-related career goals among counseling psychology doctoral students. *The Counseling Psychologist, 25*(1), 38–67.

Kapareliotis, I., Voutsina, K., & Patsiotis, A. (2019). Internship and employability prospects: Assessing student's work readiness. *Higher Education, Skills and Work-Based Learning, 9*(4), 538–549.

Kilgo, C. A., Ezell Sheets, J. K., & Pascarella, E. T. (2015). The link between high-impact practices and student learning: Some longitudinal evidence. *Higher Education, 69*, 509–525.

Kohn, M. L. (1987). Cross-national research as an analytic strategy: American Sociological Association, 1987 presidential address. *American Sociological Review, 52*(6), 713–731.

KREBS, C. J. (1991). The experimental paradigm and long-term population studies. *Ibis, 133*, 3–8.

Kuh, G. D. (2008). Excerpt from high-impact educational practices: What they are, who has access to them, and why they matter. *Association of American Colleges and Universities, 14*(3), 28–29.

References

Linn, M. C., Palmer, E., Baranger, A., Gerard, E., & Stone, E. (2015). Undergraduate research experiences: Impacts and opportunities. *Science, 347*(6222).

Lopatto, D. (2003). The essential features of undergraduate research. *Council on Undergraduate Research Quarterly, 24*(139–142).

Lopatto, D., Alvarez, C., Barnard, D., Chandrasekaran, C., Chung, H., Du, C., Eckdahl, T., Goodman, A., Hauser, C., & Jones, C. (2008). Undergraduate research. *Science, 322*(5902), 684–685.

Love, K. M., Bahner, A. D., Jones, L. N., & Nilsson, J. E. (2007). An investigation of early research experience and research self-efficacy. *Professional Psychology: Research and Practice, 38*(3), 314.

McCune, V., & Hounsell, D. (2005). The development of students' ways of thinking and practising in three final-year biology courses. *Higher Education, 49*, 255–289.

Missingham, D., Shah, S., Sabir, F., & Willison, J. (2018). Student engineers optimising problem solving and research skills. *Journal of University Teaching & Learning Practice, 15*(4), 8.

National Academies of Sciences, E., Medicine. (2017). *Undergraduate research experiences for STEM students: Successes, challenges, and opportunities*. National Academies Press.

Phillips, J. C., & Russell, R. K. (1994). Research self-efficacy, the research training environment, and research productivity among graduate students in counseling psychology. *The Counseling Psychologist, 22*(4), 628–641.

Reisberg, L. (1998). Some professors question programs that allow high-school students to earn college credits. *Chronicle of Higher Education, 44*(42).

Rowland, S. L., Lawrie, G. A., Behrendorff, J. B., & Gillam, E. M. (2012). Is the undergraduate research experience (URE) always best?: The power of choice in a bifurcated practical stream for a large introductory biochemistry class. *Biochemistry and Molecular Biology Education, 40*(1), 46–62.

Russell, S. H., Hancock, M. P., & McCullough, J. (2007). Benefits of undergraduate research experiences. *Science, 316*(5824), 548–549.

Russell, S. H., Hancock, M. P., & McCullough, J. (2007b). Benefits of undergraduate research experiences.

Seymour, E., Hunter, A. B., Laursen, S. L., & DeAntoni, T. (2004). Establishing the benefits of research experiences for undergraduates in the sciences: First findings from a three-year study. *Science Education, 88*(4), 493–534.

Shaffer, C. D., Alvarez, C. J., Bednarski, A. E., Dunbar, D., Goodman, A. L., Reinke, C., Rosenwald, A. G., Wolyniak, M. J., Bailey, C., & Barnard, D. (2014). A course-based research experience: how benefits change with increased investment in instructional time. *CBE—Life Sciences Education, 13*(1), 111–130.

Siby, N., Ammar, M., Bhadra, J., Elawad, E. F. E., Al-Thani, N. J., & Ahmad, Z. (2024). A tailored innovative model of "research internship" aimed at strengthening research competencies in STEM undergraduates. *Higher Education, Skills and Work-Based Learning*.

Spady, W. G. (1988). Organizing for results: The basis of authentic restructuring and reform. *Educational Leadership, 46*(2), 4–8.

Ward, C., Bennett, J., & Bauer, K. (2002). Content analysis of undergraduate research student evaluations. *Retrieved January, 2*, 2008.

Wass, R., Harland, T., & Mercer, A. (2011). Scaffolding critical thinking in the zone of proximal development. *Higher Education Research & Development, 30*(3), 317–328.

Wieman, C. (2017). Preparing physics students for being marooned on a desert island (and not much else). *The Physics Teacher, 55*(2), 68–68.

Willison, J., Sabir, F., & Thomas, J. (2017). Shifting dimensions of autonomy in students' research and employment. *Higher Education Research & Development, 36*(2), 430–443.

Wilmore, M., & Willison, J. (2016). Graduates' attitudes to research skill development in undergraduate media education. *Asia Pacific Media Educator, 26*(1), 113–128.

Wolkow, T. D., Jenkins, J., Durrenberger, L., Swanson-Hoyle, K., & Hines, L. M. (2019). One early course-based undergraduate research experience produces sustainable knowledge gains, but only transient perception gains. *Journal of Microbiology & Biology Education, 20*(2), https://doi.org/10.1128/jmbe.v1120i1122.1679

Open Access This chapter is licensed under the terms of the Creative Commons Attribution 4.0 International License (http://creativecommons.org/licenses/by/4.0/), which permits use, sharing, adaptation, distribution and reproduction in any medium or format, as long as you give appropriate credit to the original author(s) and the source, provide a link to the Creative Commons license and indicate if changes were made.

The images or other third party material in this chapter are included in the chapter's Creative Commons license, unless indicated otherwise in a credit line to the material. If material is not included in the chapter's Creative Commons license and your intended use is not permitted by statutory regulation or exceeds the permitted use, you will need to obtain permission directly from the copyright holder.

Chapter 6
Teaching Research to Teachers—Traversing from Research-Oriented Education to Research Learning Theory

Abstract Chapter 6 explores the pivotal role of integrating research-based methodologies into teacher education, focusing on both pre-service and in-service training. It examines how equipping teachers with research competencies can significantly influence student learning behaviors, highlighting the critical connections between effective teaching practices, professional development, and student outcomes. The chapter addresses the challenges and opportunities in cultivating a research-oriented culture within educational institutions. It advocates for a holistic approach that includes creating supportive environments, providing adequate resources, and fostering collaborative partnerships. Emphasizing the importance of integrating social-emotional learning (SEL) into teacher education programs, the chapter recognizes that teachers' social and emotional skills are essential for shaping positive classroom dynamics and creating a supportive learning atmosphere. Additionally, the chapter investigates how teachers' engagement with research impacts their instructional decisions and the development of students' autonomy and critical thinking skills. By reviewing current literature and research findings, it offers actionable insights into how schools can enhance research education training for teachers. The chapter underscores the need for continuous professional development, collaboration with research institutions, and the integration of research into teacher education curricula. Ultimately, Chapter 6 advocates for a transformative approach to teacher education, aligning with research learning theory to improve teaching effectiveness and student learning outcomes.

Keywords Teacher education · Professional development · Research-based learning in classrooms · Teacher competencies · Student learning behavior

6.1 Research-Based Teacher Education Practices

Research-based learning (RBL) is practiced in teacher education by emphasizing the use of empirical evidence and research findings to inform instructional strategies, curriculum development, and overall program improvement. RBL informs teachers to develop a deeper understanding of educational theories and best practices, allowing them to make informed decisions about their instructional approaches. It also assists them to critically analyze and evaluate existing educational research, contributing to the advancement of knowledge in the field. RBL practices adopted in teacher education ensure effective and evidence-based teaching methodologies.

Through RBL practices, teachers engage in research activities, such as investigating, refining/developing, implementing, and evaluating diverse instructional approaches. These activities are generally carried out during preservice teacher education programs through field-based or learner-teaching experiences (Maheady et al., 2002). Meanwhile, in-service teachers engage in RBL through collaborative partnerships and applied research projects wherein they enhance their professional development and improve their instructional strategies. In-service teachers apply their knowledge, and expertise to explore novel areas to improve student learning and their development. They also engage in conducting research experiments as innovative instructional methods to teach students about research and research-based activities. RBL integrated with teacher training helps to bridge the rift between theory and practice by incorporating reflective and inquiry practices into teachers' classroom-based research activities(McMillen & Fabbi, 2010). This combination of research skills and practical experience allows teachers to effectively apply evidence-based teaching strategies in their classrooms, leading to improved student achievement and overall educational outcomes. Using evidence-based teaching strategies in inclusive classrooms can also be particularly beneficial for students with disabilities, as these strategies have been shown to promote quality learning for all students, including those with disabilities (Erenand & Ali, 2017). In summary, integrated RBL encompasses equipping teachers with research skills while also acclimatizing them to the realisms of school (Saqipi & Vogrinc, 2020). These practices aim to engage teachers in ongoing professional learning and development, encourage reflective and inquiry-based practices, and foster collaborative relationships between schools and universities. Research-based learning practices in teacher education programs provide opportunities for preservice educators and practicing teachers to foster, employ, and assess instructional approaches (Maheady et al., 2002).

While RBL emphasize the importance of combining theory and practical instruction, it converges teachers towards observation and practice, and promoting collaborative research agendas among educators. It is highly reminiscent that RBL integrated teacher education guarantees higher student outcomes, as the teachers effectively transfer their acquired knowledge and expertise to foster the students. Fostering 21st century skills in students is potentially equivalent to training and empowering the respective teachers with adequate grit to flourish with the constantly changing demands of the global labor market. RBL is a very effective teaching method that vocalizes students' curiosity into inquiry, leading towards research, experimentation and interpretation, finally summarizing with meaningful dissemination, thereby building a healthy learning ecosystem. Students get easily motivated and intrigued from this practice, thereby modeling the research behavior in their learning methods resulting in improved student outcomes and overall educational excellence (McMillen & Fabbi, 2010).

Educators can become more critical consumers of educational research and evidence through RBL, making informed decisions about instructional approaches that are based on evidence and research, rather than on personal beliefs or anecdotal experience. These research-based approaches foster a culture of continuous improvement, wherein educators are encouraged to regularly reflect on their practice, seek out new research findings, and adjust their teaching strategies accordingly. They resultantly widen a deeper understanding of the subjects they teach and the best ways to instruct students. Effective integration of research and practice in teacher education programs can ensure that educators are equipped with the knowledge and dispositions needed to effectively meet the diverse needs of students in today's classrooms and readily contribute to the ongoing improvement and advancement of education.

6.2 Professional Development Experiences in Integrating Research-Based Learning in K-12 Classrooms

Diverse Professional Development (PD) programs have been launched worldwide across different educational institutes to train teachers in research and improve their research-based knowledge, skills and attitudes in different classroom settings. The NWP is a U.S.-based initiative that engages teachers with opportunities to engage in their own writing and research, fostering a culture of inquiry within classrooms. Lesson Study, program originating in Japan, is a collaborative PD approach where teachers work together to plan, observe, and analyze lessons, encouraging them to systematically examine the impact of instructional practices on student learning thereby promoting a research-oriented mindset. Harvard University initiated Research Schools International, trains teachers in research methods and in conducting and disseminating their research in a classroom-based research context. Australian Council for Educational Research (ACER) also offers PD programs for teachers that focus on research-informed practices and cover a range of topics, including assessment, data literacy, and evidence-based teaching strategies. Another initiative by the Center for Collaborative Education in the U.S. is the Teacher Research Academy that upskills teachers with the sufficient knowledge and dispositions needed to conduct action research, emphasizing collaboration and reflection. Singapore Teachers Academy for the Arts (STAA) offers PD programs for arts educators by engaging them in action research projects to enhance their teaching methods and contribute to the development of arts education. Various educational organizations implement teacher action research programs where educators under the mentorship of experienced researchers are encouraged to investigate and address specific challenges in their classrooms. In similar context, partnerships between universities and K-12 schools have successfully established teacher-researcher collaborations. These programs often involve joint projects, workshops, and ongoing support for teachers to conduct and publish research. Some successful models involve creating school-based research networks where teachers collaborate on research projects.

These networks provide a supportive environment for teachers to share insights and refine their research skills. In the United Kingdom, the Research Engaged School Award recognizes schools that actively promote research engagement among teachers. This includes supporting teachers in conducting research projects and integrating research findings into teaching practices. Research can also be taught through different approaches, that involves conferences and seminars, research projects, peer collaborative discussions, and through formal instruction offered in academic settings. Research participation is also carried out in three major modes: reading, formal tuition, and immersion. The reading mode engages researchers to explore literature mainly through reading for written tasks and/or final theses. In the tuition mode, research methods is taught through formal instruction, meanwhile immersion carries out actual research activities.

Now, as we delve into understanding the different teacher education practices that integrate or preach research, we will be exploring different PD or course programs that reveal about diverse practices and methods that teach research as well integrate them into their teaching practices. In a few studies that focused on RBL based university courses, university UG students and graduate students performed research projects over a course of semesters. The key objective of these programs as they engaged the participant student teachers included reflecting classroom practice against theories and empirical findings from school-based research. The development of adequate skills for school and teaching research were also considered to be a significant goal of the research-based study. A study based on a research based learning course (Brew & Saunders, 2020) conducted in a research intensive German university was reported to involve teachers in practitioner or action research in their ongoing PD program. This approach inculcates the development of professional competencies, expansion towards evidence-based practice, and 21st-century skills. The authors delve through the views of educators through interviews to comprehend how learning autonomy is furthered and reported that success of the PD program depends on the critical assessment of conventions about research in education and its different prospects. The study also sheds light into the challenges faced by student teachers while working on peer research projects or tutor-led research in which student engagement is hardly observed. This study was also crucial to understanding the role of decision making and its impact on research outcomes under different variables. The authors remark that implementing RBL courses faces trials in reaching a consensus on the different aspects of the research. Such a decision-making process requires critical evaluations of academics' RL experiences and the development of a grasp of how these experiences may influence their overall decisions. Furthermore, the authors suggest that the teacher educators' experiences of research influence their aptitudes to implement RBL, which raises the question of how expansive research experience may affect academics' abilities to foster learning autonomy within their students. Finally, the authors highlight that RBL passes an emancipatory agenda, but the relative nature of rationality must be considered when implementing such programs. These findings in fact direct towards the relationship between the environmental factors and the student learning outcomes as posited by the RCT.

6.2 Professional Development Experiences in Integrating Research-Based ...

The study used the RBL decision making wheel model (see Fig. 6.1) as a lens for a innate insight of decision-making in RBL integrated teacher education. By examining how teacher educators respond to the challenge of implementing a RBL course and what effects their teaching strategies have, the authors evaluate the contribution of the research to acknowledging the execution of RBL in teacher education and probe the inferences for the Wheel Model. The authors argue that analytical investigation by teacher educators of their past RL experiences is a criterion for realistic decision-making and suggest that the Wheel Model can play a key role in supporting this reflection process. From this research course the participants also fostered a reflective attitude in the context of the research practice. Examining the reflective attitude of the participants was also performed by a study on the perceptions of teacher educators towards research practices conducted in Netherlands. Upon surveying 508 teacher educators and interviewing 10 educators, further insights were gathered on their perceptions towards research, their apparent capabilities to carry out research, and the pre-requisite for support (Willemse & Boei, 2013). The article was an impetus with emphasis on the participant teachers' outlook on research, listing their attitudes towards conducting research, barriers and facilitators, research skills and training, research dissemination, and the resultant relationship between research and teaching, augmenting the quality of teaching and credibility as perceived by the students. Educators emphasize the need for societies of inquiry through which they can collaborate on research, bolster their skills, foster a ground language, and resultantly contribute to the knowledge in teacher education. According to the study, research plays an important role in teacher education as it contributes to the development of teachers and their teaching practice, adds to the knowledge base of the profession, introduces new teachers to the world of inquiry, and improves the curriculum for teacher education and the preparation of new teachers.

Another study by Reis-Jorge (2005) employs a case study to demonstrate an alternative approach to relating the process of research in linking with diverse types of research based knowledge likely to be established and attained by student teachers as they perform different means of engagement in research in formal contexts of instruction. The student teachers carry out critical reflection, action research, case study, and self-study, among others, that formed the foundations to the development of a five-level framework for teacher research and professional development. The framework was developed based on both quantitative and qualitative data collected from three questionnaires directed to the teachers at distinct stages of the course, in addition to their interviews and observation of their activities. The framework thus developed will offer a systematic and transformative approach to PD in research for teachers that seeks to engage them in the research process and support them in acquiring the necessary knowledge and skills to carry out research in their own practice. The framework comprises different pillars that mold the foundation for the research-based knowledge and skill development—(1) Building awareness and understanding, (2) Developing skills and competencies, (3) Building capacity and confidence, and (4) Enhancing impact and sustainability. However, this framework does not leave room to address the lack of teacher's confidence in performing a research activity or the limited prospects for PD for teachers in research.

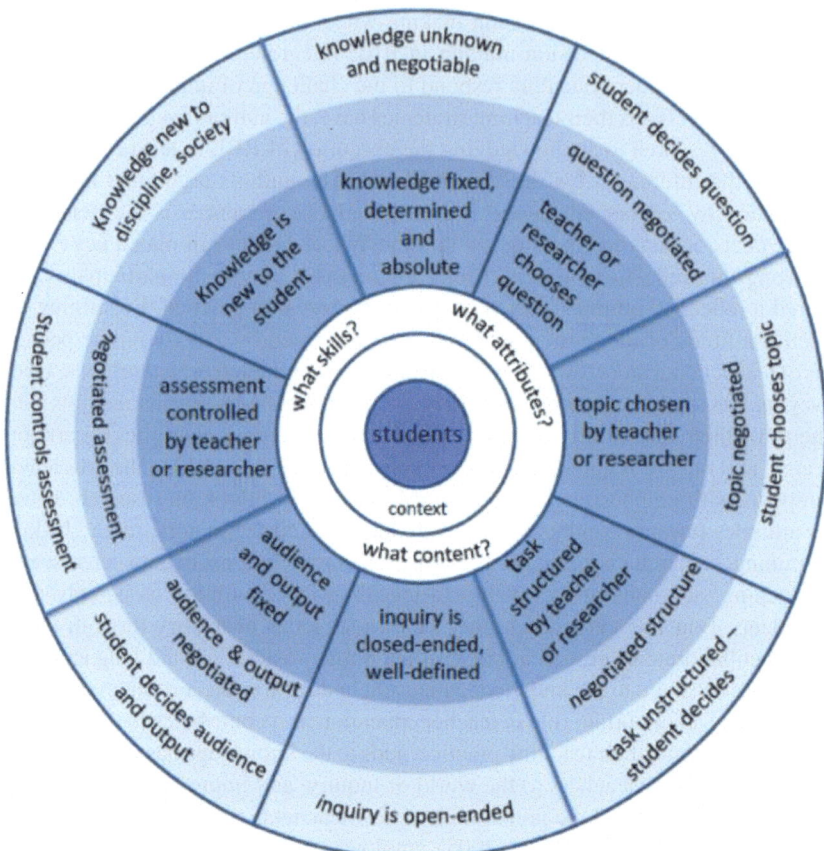

Fig. 6.1 RBL decision-making wheel. This provides a framework for aligning teaching strategies with research-based learning objectives. It illustrates the dynamic interplay between content, skills, and attributes in the RBL process, highlighting the levels of student agency and teacher guidance. The model emphasizes varying degrees of structure, inquiry, and student involvement to accommodate diverse learning contexts and objectives. Reproduced with permission from (Brew & Saunders, 2020).

While addressing relevant literature related to developing teachers' positive attitudes from a research environment, study by van der Linden, W. and team (2012) offers significant evidences that reliable learning tasks with cases from practice and collaborative work were found to be the most effective methods to develop positive research attitudes on research skills, knowledge and behavior (van der Linden et al., 2012). This findings falls directly under the RCT, where a dynamic research environment under social influence has the ability to construct the research behavior of an individual. Here, the key environmental features that contributed to the effectiveness of the course are as follows:

1. Context-specific and practice-oriented problems associated with teaching practice;
2. Interest and accountability to upgrade PD and teaching performance;
3. Problem based teaching practice;
4. Reflective and Research-oriented learner attitude;

This study measured the cognitive, behavioral, and affective, aspects of attitude towards research, which indeed was an outcomes calibrated from the aforementioned environmental features. Moreover, a socio-constructivist perspective on learning was introduced in the course content, whereby learners collaboratively construct their intrinsic knowledge in dynamic situations. Though the above-mentioned studies enlighten us on the different research skill development approaches and reflective learning, impact of situations or environment is not discussed to reflect the process of RL. i.e., the realities of implementing the research taught in school classrooms and the process of addressing each research activity while reflecting the outcomes on the basis of theories is hardly discussed.

However, the study by Worrall (2004) investigates the limitations and complexities of advocating a school-wide research culture. The study investigates teachers' research beliefs, and their research attitudes on developing research skills. Through interviews with participant teachers, the article features realistic strategies for warranting teaching as a research-informed profession. This study stresses promoting teacher engagement in research activity, by creating a dynamic research environment, which is crucial to developing the resultant research beliefs and attitudes. This feature of the study leads to the emergence of the RCT that focuses on the development of research behavior on the basis of situation and research environment. The study also emphasis on running access to relevant teaching resources, building effective research questions, and strong research collaborations, leading to extensive dissemination and sharing of research findings, offering recognition and extrinsic motivation to the teachers. It is also significant to grant teachers with ample time and opportunities to carry out research, develop a research culture, thereby promoting collaboration and reflection. The study also converges towards the necessity to investigate teachers' motivations and research beliefs, based on their practice, harvesting information, and observing, and interpreting the results. The study also raises the limitations of carrying out research in school classroom in the context of exercised methods and techniques. This may vary depending on a scale of factors, including the type or requisite of the research question raised, the available resources, and the inherent skills in both students and teachers. Some of the key challenges in practicing school research include lack of time, skepticism on the ability to perform research, such as cornering research for only highly intellectual students and teachers, negative research attitudes, personal dispositions and institutional barriers such as a lack of laboratory/experimental resources, etc. Another similar study was conducted by Lovat, T. and his colleagues (1995) investigating and examining the effects of integrating RSD in teacher education programs, with the aim of generating reflective, inquiry-based practicing teachers (Lovat et al., 1995). This study was focused on an intervention that integrated research outlining different skills that were a part of the school curriculum. Inquiry based research problems under the "action research" model, were introduced during the program, where each teacher explores their own situation to get a deeper conception of the teaching process. The objective of this model is to build a stark knowledge base upon which teachers can interpret and more readily incorporate research findings into their classrooms.

Another study that focuses on the different pathways that determine teachers' research attitudes and skills is also closely associated with emerging the RCT (Ulanoff et al., 2003). The study reports on the experiences of 45 in-service teachers enrolled in an MA in Education program as they perform research activities and foster an inquiry ethic while collecting and analyzing data, socializing (collaborating) with instructors and peers, being motivated to engage in inquiry driven dialogue, and deriving conclusions from their findings during a semester-long course. During the research course teachers accomplished informal reflections about their research on a weekly basis and formal reflections in the form of an open-ended survey. Teachers also involve in reflection during class meetings with peers and instructors during class discussions and join in in writing groups that meet weekly as a regular class activity where they share feedback about the inquiry projects. The feedback offered by the instructors guide them in developing their research reflections. According to the authors, research is dependent upon the actual classroom teaching and teacher research has a vital role in supplementing to the knowledge base of teaching and learning, and that the relationship between teaching and research is a reciprocal one, which clearly calls out the RCT statement.

6.3 How Can Schools Support the Promotion of Research Education Training of Teachers?

Research capacity in teacher education is crucial for the development of a high-quality educational system. It not only enhances the teaching practices of educators but also nurtures an environment where teachers can act as public intellectuals and change agents. While this is recognized across Europe and North America, the field of teacher education also faces specific challenges in developing research capacity (Murray et al., 2008). The impact of research on teacher performance and student learning is evident, motivating educators to initiate new projects and sustain their impact (Zhou & Liu, 2019). Moreover, professionals in teaching should evolve through research to gain a deeper understanding of effective teacher PD and education. This involves research on teachers' knowledge, skills, and attitudes toward collaborative, inquiry-based, and contextualized education, as well as the development and assessment of programs and interventions fostering collaborative learning. Prospective teachers bring their preconceived beliefs and assumptions about teaching and learning from their own schooling experiences, making teacher education programs an influential space for shaping these perspectives. By collaborating with creativity researchers, teacher educators can identify and disseminate insights to help teachers adopt classroom practices that nurture students' creative potential (Menter, 2021). The need for research capacity in teacher education is clear, and schools can play a pivotal role in supporting this endeavor by creating a culture of inquiry, providing resources, fostering collaborations, integrating research into teacher education programs, and recognizing and celebrating the research. Schools play a crucial role in supporting the promotion of research education training for teachers (Junger et al., 2017).

Promoting a culture of research and providing opportunities for professional development, schools can empower teachers to engage in research and enhance their teaching practices (Lovat et al., 1995). This can be achieved through a variety of approaches, including offering comprehensive workshops and training sessions on research methods and techniques aimed at empowering teachers to enhance their research skills. The schools also can ensure access to resources such as research journals, databases, and literature that assist in facilitating relevant and rigorous research endeavors for teachers. They can establish collaborations with universities, research institutions, and other educational organizations to foster partnerships that open doors for teachers to actively participate in meaningful research projects. Integrating components dedicated to conducting research into teacher education programs such as incorporating courses on research methods or implementing capstone projects mandating teachers to formulate and execute their own comprehensive studies is a very promising aspect of school engagement. Schools may also create a supportive and collaborative environment where teachers can share their research findings, learn from each other's experiences, and receive feedback and support from colleagues and mentors. In doing so, schools can foster a culture of continuous improvement and evidence-based practice, where teachers are encouraged to critically reflect on their teaching strategies and implement innovative approaches based on research evidence.

Teachers need support for research education training from schools to ensure they have the knowledge, skills, and resources necessary to engage in research. This support can come in the form of dedicated time for research, access to funding or grants for research projects, and mentorship from experienced researchers or faculty (Ulanoff et al., 2003). Additionally, schools can provide opportunities for teachers to present their research findings at conferences or publish their work in professional journals, further contributing to the dissemination of knowledge and the professional growth of teachers. In sum, schools can support the promotion of research education training for teachers by nurturing research culture, allocating resources and access to research materials, fostering collaboration and partnerships, integrating research into teacher education programs, and recognizing and celebrating the research efforts and achievements of teachers (Zhou & Liu, 2019).

Prior research elaborates on the role of schools wherein they can support the promotion of research education training of teachers by allocating considerable time to examine teacher educators' practices and enhance research capacity within the university (Willemse & Boei, 2013). The establishment of a culture of research depends on supporting the development of a shared language and vision on research as built by the schools, which is important for both teacher educators and student teachers. Within communities of inquiry, teacher educators might be able to develop a shared language, vision, and a shared support system for student teachers. Additionally, specific and practical strategies need to be implemented to ensure that teaching as a research-informed profession can become a reality. The Teacher Training Agency's work in encouraging research activity and the Best Practice Research Scholarship (BPRS) scheme are examples of government funding being used to stimulate teachers to engage in research activity (Worrall, 2004). Puustinen et al. (2018) found that teacher candidates who had experienced research-based teacher education, alongside practical teaching, argued for the benefits of this kind of program (Puustinen et al., 2018). Schools can, therefore, consider supporting the incorporation of research-based programs into their existing teacher education curricula, to help support the promotion of research education training for their future teaching staff. In doing so, schools can create an opportunity for teachers to develop and reflect on their own practice, in addition to potentially improving teacher retention rates (Brew & Saunders, 2020). Teacher education institutes play a fundamental role in developing curricula that instruct student teachers in the skills of conducting research and applying findings from other research (van der Linden et al., 2012). This can be achieved by providing courses that foster students' acknowledgment that engaging in and applying research is an integral aspect of the teaching profession.

Decades ago, Lawrence Stenhouse recognized the interconnection among teacher inquiry, professional development, and school enhancement. Stenhouse underscored the significance of curriculum development as the most fruitful domain for endeavors in this regard (Baumfield, 2006). While control over the school curriculum has transitioned from teachers to centralized governing bodies, educators still wield influence over the pedagogical methods employed in the classroom. Teachers engaged in integrating thinking skills into the curriculum often cite the restoration of a sense of professional autonomy as a significant motivational factor. The systematic review conducted by the Evidence for Policy and Practice Information and Co-ordinating Centre (EPPI) suggests that infusing thinking skills into the curriculum serves as a focal point for developing pedagogy that both stimulates and supports practitioner inquiry. Consequently, schools can facilitate the advancement of teachers' research education training by incorporating a focus on thinking skills in the curriculum. This approach enables a social constructivist learning model shared by both pupils and teachers, fostering the creation of a critical community of practice.

A prior investigation explores an alternative method for delineating the research process in relation to various forms of research knowledge that student teachers are likely to acquire and cultivate through diverse modes of research engagement within formal instructional settings (Reis-Jorge, 2005). This description could serve as a foundation for studies focused on teacher involvement in research or as an instructional instrument and roadmap for crafting teaching and learning activities within research methods courses for educators. Consequently, schools have the potential to furnish such instructional aids and engage teachers in research as an integral component of their professional development.

6.4 Relationship Between Teacher Competencies and Student Learning Behavior in the Context of Research Learning

As we delve into the intricate connection between teacher competencies and student learning behavior, it is essential to understand the impact of professional development on teaching practices and student outcomes. The effectiveness of teachers in fostering student learning is often linked to their competencies and behavior in the classroom, as well as their ability to utilize multiple learning resources for instructional purposes. Teachers who are adept at monitoring expectations, providing clear objectives, encouraging student participation, and offering constructive feedback create an environment conducive to student learning and growth (Hartono, 2017). The evidence-based prior research also highlights the influence of teacher competencies on students' social-emotional learning, emphasizing the importance of teachers' awareness of their emotions and relationships within the classroom (Harsoyo et al., 2019; Pangalila et al., 2018). Furthermore, the influence of teacher competencies on students' learning achievement has been a focal point of numerous studies. Understanding the correlation between teacher competencies and student outcomes contributes significantly to the development of effective teaching practices and educational policies. In light of these research findings, it becomes evident that exploring the dynamics of teacher competencies and their impact on student learning behavior is crucial for shaping the future of education and empowering educators to create impactful learning environments.

Educators and educational institutions must recognize the importance of professional development and the role it plays in enhancing teacher competencies and student outcomes. By prioritizing the development of pedagogical, professional, and social competencies among teachers, we can ensure that students receive a high-quality education that promotes holistic growth and development. With a focus on enhancing teacher competencies, it is imperative to address the gaps in pre-service and in-service teacher education. Research has shown that teacher social and emotional competence significantly impacts the effectiveness of social-emotional learning (SEL) programs in schools. It is crucial to integrate SEL content into teacher education standards, ensuring that teachers are equipped with comprehensive SEL competencies to effectively support students' socio-emotional development.

Moreover, the link between teacher competencies and the quality of teacher-student relationships cannot be overlooked. Teachers' social-emotional competence influences the dynamic interactions within the classroom, shaping students' attitudes towards learning and their overall academic experience. Therefore, investing in the development of teachers' social and emotional skills is a strategic approach towards creating a conducive and supportive learning environment.

In parallel to professional development initiatives, the integration of social-emotional learning into teacher preparation policies and curricula holds immense promise. By equipping pre-service teachers with a deep understanding of child and adolescent development, educators can lay a strong foundation for the acquisition of social-emotional competence and the improvement of student learning outcomes. This forward-looking approach not only enhances the capacity of teachers to address the diverse needs of their students but also fosters a more comprehensive and holistic approach to education.

As we navigate the landscape of professional development and teacher competencies, it is imperative to extend our focus to both pre-service and in-service teacher education. The integration of comprehensive SEL competencies into teacher education standards can serve as a catalyst for transformative change in the education sector. By addressing the critical need for teachers to develop their own social and emotional skills, educational institutions can effectively nurture a culture of empathy, understanding, and collaboration within the classroom setting.

As Puustinen et al. (2018) suggest, the way a teacher engages with research—whether as a consumer, an applier of existing research, or a practitioner-researcher—can vary and influence the development of students' autonomy through research-based learning. In turn, the extent to which students can apply what they have learned from such research is likely to be variable, as individual teacher educators may focus on aspects of research based on their self experiences and potentially ignore or downplay other aspects. According to the van der Linden and his colleagues, teacher research can play a significant role in improving student learning outcomes as teachers who carry out research are attentive of the significance of critical self-reflection and self-evaluation, the aptitude to observe, analyze and interpret the behavior and learning results of students, and teacher accountability (van der Linden et al., 2012). Studies demonstrate that when teachers have research skills, they are more likely to use a thinking-skills approach in their teaching, which leads to greater student responsibility and autonomy (Baumfield, 2006). Through a focus on thinking skills, students are encouraged to articulate and discuss their ideas while understanding is negotiated. As teachers gain new perception into the thinking of their learners, this often leads to a shift in the teachers' attention, resulting in a refocusing of priorities and a greater focus on the underlying concepts and processes. While teaching using a thinking-skills approach can be demanding, the benefits include the promotion of teacher inquiry, teaching changes, and improved student learning outcomes. Studies by Ulanoff and his colleagues emphasizes the importance of teacher research and inquiry-based instruction in engaging students in the learning process (Ulanoff et al., 2003). Through inquiry-based instruction, teachers can better connect with their students and be more attuned to their learning needs. Additionally, by engaging in their own inquiry projects, teachers can become better instructional decision-makers, which can ultimately lead to better student learning outcomes.

Conversely, Reis-Jorge's study (2005) explores the insufficient focus on how student teachers acquire knowledge about research and the impact this has on their perception of themselves as inquisitive professionals, especially among those for whom research is a novel aspect of their education (Reis-Jorge, 2005). Conventional avenues of acquiring knowledge about research often portray various research methodologies as prepackaged sets of techniques for students to select, akin to choosing software like Word to compose their final output. Therefore, it can be inferred that teachers with deeper research knowledge and skills might be capable of providing better research learning. Appendix C shows how competencies translate to tangible impacts on student behavior. Therefore, the research skills of a teacher educator may impact how students' learning behavior develops through such research-based learning. However, more research is needed to understand the explicit relationship between teacher's research skills and student learning behavior.

6.5 Chapter Summary

In this chapter, we explore how research can be effectively integrated into teacher education, emphasizing the importance of equipping educators with the skills and mindset needed to foster research-based learning in classrooms. Research-based learning (RBL) in teacher education involves engaging educators in research activities, bridging theory and practice, and fostering reflective and inquiry-driven approaches. By embedding research within both preservice and in-service training, teachers develop the capacity to critically evaluate educational practices, apply evidence-based methodologies, and create innovative learning environments. RBL equips educators to address diverse classroom needs and enhances their ability to foster 21st-century skills in students, resulting in improved educational outcomes. This chapter highlights the pivotal role of RBL in fostering educators' professional growth and enriching their pedagogical approaches.

The discussion extends to professional development (PD) programs that integrate research practices, showcasing global initiatives like the U.S.-based National Writing Project and Japan's Lesson Study. These programs aim to enhance teachers' research skills through collaborative projects, action research, and partnerships with educational institutions. Examples such as Harvard's Research Schools International and Singapore's Teachers Academy for the Arts illustrate how structured PD programs nurture a research-oriented mindset among educators. Furthermore, frameworks like the RBL decision-making wheel model provide insights into implementing RBL effectively, emphasizing the interplay between teacher autonomy, reflective practice, and research-informed decision-making. These efforts underline the transformative potential of research-based PD in cultivating a culture of inquiry within schools, empowering teachers to explore, evaluate, and innovate in their instructional practices.

The chapter concludes by exploring the dynamic relationship between teacher competencies and student learning behavior within a research-driven context. It emphasizes the critical role of professional development in enhancing teachers' pedagogical and social-emotional competencies, directly impacting classroom dynamics and student outcomes. By fostering a culture of inquiry, supporting collaborative research, and integrating social-emotional learning into teacher education, schools can empower educators to inspire autonomy, critical thinking, and curiosity among students. Research highlights the reciprocal relationship between teacher inquiry and student learning, advocating for a holistic approach where educators and learners engage in mutual growth through research-based practices. Through this lens, the chapter underscores the importance of creating robust support systems, reflective practices, and innovative strategies to bridge research and pedagogy, thereby shaping a more impactful and future-ready education system.

Glossary

Term Definition

Research-Based Learning (RBL) A pedagogical approach that integrates research into teaching, enabling educators to critically evaluate and apply evidence-based strategies.

Professional Development (PD) Ongoing training programs designed to enhance teachers' knowledge, skills, and competencies in their professional roles.

Action Research A reflective process where educators investigate specific challenges in their classrooms to improve teaching and learning practices.

Lesson Study A collaborative PD method originating in Japan, where teachers jointly plan, observe, and analyze lessons to refine instructional practices.

National Writing Project (NWP) A U.S.-based initiative that engages teachers in writing and research to promote a culture of inquiry in classrooms.

Reflective Practice The process by which educators analyze their teaching experiences to improve their methods and outcomes.

RBL Decision-Making Wheel Model A framework aligning teaching strategies with RBL objectives, emphasizing the balance between teacher guidance and student autonomy.

Inquiry-Based Learning (IBL) An educational strategy where students and teachers engage in exploring questions, problems, and scenarios to foster deep understanding.

Social-Emotional Learning (SEL) Programs that develop self-awareness, emotional regulation, and interpersonal skills, enhancing both teacher and student outcomes.

21st-Century Skills Competencies such as critical thinking, creativity, collaboration, and communication essential for success in modern education and careers.

Teacher-Researcher Collaboration Partnerships between educators and researchers to conduct studies and apply findings to improve teaching practices.

Thinking-Skills Approach A teaching method emphasizing critical thinking, problem-solving, and reflective inquiry in student learning.

Research Capacity The ability of educators and institutions to engage in, support, and apply educational research effectively.

School-Based Research Networks Collaborative platforms where teachers and researchers work together on educational studies to share insights and refine practices.

Research Self-Efficacy Confidence in one's ability to conduct and apply research effectively in educational contexts.

Socio-Constructivist Perspective A learning theory emphasizing knowledge construction through social interaction and collaboration.

Dynamic Research Environment An interactive, supportive setting fostering active learning, inquiry, and collaboration among teachers and students.

Teacher Inquiry A reflective process where educators investigate their teaching practices to enhance their effectiveness and student learning.

Research Learning Theory (RCT) A framework emphasizing the interaction between social contexts, dynamic learning environments, and cognitive behavior in research.

Collaborative Professional Learning A PD approach where educators work together to solve problems, develop strategies, and share insights for improved teaching.

Research Engagement Active involvement in research activities, from designing studies to applying findings, to enhance teaching and learning outcomes.

Best Practice Research Scholarship (BPRS) A program encouraging teachers to engage in research activities, contributing to professional growth and improved student outcomes.

Capstone Project A culminating research project in teacher education programs where educators design and implement studies to address classroom challenges.

References

Baumfield, V. (2006). Tools for pedagogical inquiry: The impact of teaching thinking skills on teachers. *Oxford Review of Education, 32*(02), 185–196.

Brew, A., & Saunders, C. (2020). Making sense of research-based learning in teacher education. *Teaching and Teacher Education, 87*, 102935.

Erenand, E. O., & Ali, N. A. B. N. (2017). Evidence-based practice: Inclusive education for the effective implementation for children with autism. In *Proceedings of the International Conference on Education* (Vol. 3, No. 1, pp. 114–128).

Harsoyo, Y., Astuti, C. W. R., & Rahayu, C. W. E. (2019). Competency and values of local wisdom of high school principals. *Jurnal Cakrawala Pendidikan, 38*(3), 565–577.

Hartono, M. (2017). Model of supervision based on primary school teacher professional competency in Tematic learning in curriculum 2013. *Journal of Education Research and Evaluation, 1*(3), 162–167.

Junger, J., Kačúr, P., Tlučáková, L., Čech, P., & Bebčáková, V. (2017). Physical activity of female students in secondary schools in the context of physical activity recommendations fulfilment. *Human Movement, 18*(3), 67–73.

Lovat, T., Davies, M., & Plotnikoff, R. (1995). Integrating research skills development in teacher education. *Australian Journal of Teacher Education, 20*(1), 30–35.

Maheady, L., Michielli-Pendl, J., Mallette, B., & Harper, G. F. (2002). A collaborative research project to improve the academic performance of a diverse sixth grade science class. *Teacher Education and Special Education, 25*(1), 55–70.

McMillen, P., & Fabbi, J. (2010). How to be an E3 librarian. *Public Services Quarterly, 6*(2–3), 174–186.

Menter, I. (2021). Teacher education research: Values-based planning in an uncertain world. *Образование и Саморазвитие, 16*(3), 158–166.

Murray, J., Campbell, A., Hextall, I., Hulme, M., Jones, M., Mahony, P., Menter, I., Procter, R., & Wall, K. (2008). Mapping the field of teacher education research: Methodology and issues in a research capacity building initiative in teacher education in the United Kingdom. *European Educational Research Journal, 7*(4), 459–474.

Pangalila, T., Pasandaran, S., & Lonto, A. L. (2018). Emotional quotient, family environment and their influences on teacher performance. In *Annual Civic Education Conference (ACEC 2018)* (pp. 124–127). Atlantis Press

Puustinen, M., Säntti, J., Koski, A., & Tammi, T. (2018). Teaching: A practical or research-based profession? Teacher candidates' approaches to research-based teacher education. *Teaching and Teacher Education, 74*, 170–179.

Reis-Jorge, J. M. (2005). Developing teachers' knowledge and skills as researchers: A conceptual framework. *Asia-Pacific Journal of Teacher Education, 33*(3), 303–319.

Saqipi, B., & Vogrinc, J. (2020). The development of teacher research as a form of developing teacher pedagogical practice. *Center for Educational Policy Studies Journal, 10*(3), 5–9.

Ulanoff, S. H., Vega-Castaneda, L., & Quiocho, A. M. (2003). Teachers as researchers: Developing an inquiry ethic. *Teacher Development, 7*(3), 403–435.

van der Linden, W., Bakx, A., Ros, A., Beijaard, D., & Vermeulen, M. (2012). Student teachers' development of a positive attitude towards research and research knowledge and skills. *European Journal of Teacher Education, 35*(4), 401–419.

Willemse, T., & Boei, F. (2013). Teacher educators' research practices: An explorative study of teacher educators' perceptions on research. *Journal of Education for Teaching, 39*(4), 354–369.

Worrall, N. (2004). Trying to build a research culture in a school: Trying to find the right questions to ask. *Teacher Development, 8*(2–3), 137–148.

Zhou, H., & Liu, X. (2019). Narrative research on the professional development of PE teachers. In *2nd International Workshop on Education Reform and Social Sciences* (ERSS 2019) (pp. 217–220). Atlantis Press.

Open Access This chapter is licensed under the terms of the Creative Commons Attribution 4.0 International License (http://creativecommons.org/licenses/by/4.0/), which permits use, sharing, adaptation, distribution and reproduction in any medium or format, as long as you give appropriate credit to the original author(s) and the source, provide a link to the Creative Commons license and indicate if changes were made.

The images or other third party material in this chapter are included in the chapter's Creative Commons license, unless indicated otherwise in a credit line to the material. If material is not included in the chapter's Creative Commons license and your intended use is not permitted by statutory regulation or exceeds the permitted use, you will need to obtain permission directly from the copyright holder.

Appendices

Appendix A: Stages of the CURE Model and Their Impact on Undergraduate Learners

CURE Stage	Key activities	Skills developed	Impact on learners
Orientation	Introduction to research concepts	Familiarity with research process	Builds confidence and aligns expectations
	Setting research objectives	Goal setting	
	Overview of expected outcomes		
Inquiry and Problem Framing	Posing research questions	Critical thinking	Encourages curiosity and analytical abilities
	Designing experimental methods	Problem-solving	
Data Collection	Conducting experiments	Observational skills	Reinforces hands-on learning and methodical approaches
	Collecting quantitative/qualitative data	Technical expertise	
Data Analysis and Synthesis	Analyzing results using statistical or computational tools	Analytical reasoning	Deepens understanding of research methodologies and interpretation of findings
	Synthesizing findings into cohesive conclusions	Interpretation skills	
Dissemination of Findings	Writing research papers	Communication	Develops presentation skills and professional readiness
	Presenting results in seminars or conferences	Public speaking	

(continued)

(continued)

CURE Stage	Key activities	Skills developed	Impact on learners
Reflection and Feedback	Reviewing challenges and successes	Reflective practice	Promotes self-improvement and adaptability
	Revising research practices based on feedback	Resilience	

Appendix B: Key Components of Research Cognitive Theory (RCT) and Their Educational Applications

Component	Description	Application in educational context
Self-efficacy	The belief that an individual has in demonstrating a behavior	Encouraging students to engage in independent inquiry by building confidence in their abilities
Behavioral Capability	Understanding and having the ability to execute a behavior	Teaching students the stepbystep process of designing experiments and solving problems
Expectations	Defining the effects of the desired behavior	Setting clear objectives for research activities and aligning student efforts with tangible outcomes
Expectancies	Transferring value to the outcomes of desired behavior	Linking research skills to realworld applications and future career prospects to motivate students
Self-control	Regulating and observing an individual's behavior	Training students in time management and goalsetting for longterm projects or research tasks
Observational Learning	Observing the behavior of others and performing or modeling the desired behavior	Facilitating peer collaboration and mentorship programs to enable learning through observation
Reinforcements	Endorsing incentives and rewards that promote the desired behavior	Providing rewards such as certifications, recognition, or tangible outcomes to reinforce learning

Appendix C: Teacher Competencies and Impact on Student Learning Behaviors

Teacher competency	Description	Impact on student learning behavior	Examples of integration in RBL context
Pedagogical Skills	Proficiency in structuring and delivering engaging lessons tailored to diverse student needs	Increases student engagement and participation	Using real-world examples in inquiry-based lessons
		Improves conceptual understanding	Breaking complex problems into manageable steps
Research Skills	Ability to guide students in inquiry, data collection, analysis, and synthesis	Encourages curiosity and critical thinking	Guiding students in designing experiments
		Develops problem-solving skills	Teaching data interpretation techniques
Social-Emotional Competence	Awareness and regulation of emotions, fostering positive teacher-student relationships	Enhances collaboration and motivation	Encouraging teamwork through group projects
		Builds a safe and inclusive learning environment	Providing emotional support during challenging tasks
Communication Skills	Clear, precise, and empathetic communication with students and colleagues	Improves clarity of concepts	Facilitating meaningful discussions
		Enhances student ability to articulate ideas and ask questions	Encouraging students to present research findings
Assessment Literacy	Proficiency in designing, interpreting, and using assessments to improve learning	Promotes reflective learning and self-assessment	Developing rubrics for research projects
		Tracks skill progression over time	Offering formative feedback during inquiry activities
Technological Competence	Ability to integrate digital tools to enhance teaching and research learning	Broadens access to information	Utilizing online databases for research
		Facilitates collaboration and innovation	Teaching data visualization tools like Excel or Python

The manufacturer's authorised representative in the EU is Springer Nature Customer Service Centre GmbH, Europaplatz 3, 69115 Heidelberg, Germany. If you have any concerns regarding our products, please contact ProductSafety@springernature.com

Printed and bound by CPI Group (UK) Ltd, Croydon, CR0 4YY

23/03/2026

02076360-0015